Art of Chainsaw Carving

by Jessie Groeschen

High Country Chorus by J. Chester Armstrong

Fox Chapel Publishing

1970 Broad Street • East Petersburg, PA 17520
www.FoxChapelPublishing.com

Alan Giagnocavo
PUBLISHER

Peg Couch
ACQUISITION EDITOR

Gretchen Bacon
EDITOR

Troy Thorne
DESIGN & LAYOUT

Art of Chainsaw Carving is an original work, first published in 2005 by Fox Chapel Publishing Company, Inc. No part of this book may be duplicated for resale or distribution under any circumstances. Any such copying is a violation of copyright law.

Pat McVay's profile contains a slightly revised version of "Legendary Wood Carver Pat McVay." *The Ticket* (April 2005), reprinted with permission of the author of the article.

Don Colp's profile contains a slightly revised version of "Don Colp, Judge's Biography." *West Coast, The Big One!*, reprinted with permission of the author of the biography.

ISBN-10: 1–56523–250–X
ISBN-13: 978–1–56523–250–1

Publisher's Cataloging-in-Publication Data

Groeschen, Jessie.

    Art of chainsaw carving / by Jessie Groeschen. -- East Petersburg,
PA : Fox Chapel Publishing, c2005.

      p. ; cm.

      ISBN-13: 978-1-56523-250-1
      ISBN-10: 1-56523-250-X
      Includes bibliographical references.

      1. Wood-carving--Technique. 2. Wood-carving--Patterns.
    3. Wood sculpture. 4. Chain saws. I. Title.

TT199.7 .G76 2005
736/.4--dc22   0509

Interior photography by Jessie Groeschen except where noted.
Cover artwork by J. Chester Armstrong
Cover photography by Brent McGragor
Year of the Dragon on back cover by Glenn Greensides
Tree Frog on back cover by Brian Ruth
Sun, Moon, Bear Chair on back cover by Jessie Groeschen

To learn more about the other great books from Fox Chapel Publishing, or to find a
retailer near you, call toll-free 1-800-457-9112 or visit us at
www.FoxChapelPublishing.com.

Printed in the United States of America
10 9 8 7 6 5 4 3 2 1

Note to Authors: We are always looking for talented authors to write new books in our area of woodworking, design, and related crafts. Please send a brief letter describing your idea to

Peg Couch, Acquisition Editor,
1970 Broad Street, East Petersburg, PA 17520

Because carving wood and other materials inherently includes the risk of injury and damage, this book cannot guarantee that creating the projects in this book is safe for everyone. For this reason, this book is sold without warranties or guarantees of any kind, expressed or implied, and the publisher and the author disclaim any liability for any injuries, losses, or damages caused in any way by the content of this book or the reader's use of the tools needed to complete the projects presented here. The publisher and the author urge all carvers to thoroughly review each project and to understand the use of all tools before beginning any project.

Dedication

For my mother, Guadalupe Lourdes Sunio Groeschen
As I was carving my reflections of the universe
Around us in Western Red Cedar
While working on the evening sky,
She said,
"Keep putting more stars in"

Acknowledgments

I would like to express my gratitude to all of the artists and carvers who shared their work with me. Without their patience, friendship, and talent, this book would not exist. Thank you to Bailey's, **www.baileys-online.com**, for always listening to what I had to say. I would also like to thank Golden Eagle Distributing, **www.goldeneagledist.com**, for providing me with saws over the years. Thanks to Husqvarna for their recent support, **www.husqvarna.com**. I would like to recognize Nick Worsfold for loaning me his computer and Greg Groeschen for suiting the computer to my needs. Also, thanks to my family. A very special thank you goes to Ms. Nordhoff of Whidbey Island, Washington, for her support. Thanks also to Pat McVay for his many photos and recollections of many events of the past and for his enthusiasm about art and woodcarving. Additionally, I would like to thank Susan Miller for her keen insights in matters of art, woodcarving, and life, and I cannot adequately express my gratitude to Lois Hollingsworth for saying the word "believe"—thank you, Lois. Most of all, I would like to thank the Creator of nature; the Earth is a wonderful gift.

❖ Contents ❖

About the Author

▲ Jessie posing with *My Feminine.*

Jessie Groeschen

Jessie Groeschen is a professional artist who has competed in over 30 extreme chainsaw and power sculpting contests. Her home is in the Pacific Northwest. She is an active member of the Artists' Cooperative Gallery of Whidbey Island, Washington. In 2002, she took her art to Toei, Japan, becoming the first foreigner to compete in Japan's Chainsaw Carving Championships; she created *Three Stages of the Rose.* In 2003, Jessie earned first place in the premier Women in Art: Chainsaw Series. Jessie was the first woman to place in the top 10 of the Judges' Choice category at the nation's largest chainsaw competition, West Coast, The Big One!, with her carving *Broken Seashell.* Jessie has also competed in the first English Open Chainsaw Caving Championships and was recognized by Seattle's Folklife Festival in a group exhibit. Her work has been featured on national media outlets, such as ESPN. In addition to carving, Jessie also writes to promote chainsaw carving as an art form. In 1993, she co-founded *The Cutting Edge* newsletter for the Cascade Chainsaw Sculptors Guild; Jessie served as the editor of the newsletter from 1993 to 2000 and has also written articles for *Chip Chats* and *Woodcarving UK.* This is her first book.

◀ *My Feminine.* Sitka spruce, 6' tall by 2' wide, 1995. Photo by Ed Severinghaus. The author carved this piece in the West Coast, The Big One!, and then took it home and finished up. "I had no idea what I was carving, it just emerged," Jessie says.

Jessie Groeschen

▲ *Icarus and Daedalus.* Madrona, 4' tall by 2' wide, 1998. This piece is Jessie's interpretation of the famous myth.

▲ Jessie nicking off a burr on *Sun Chasing the Moon.* Western red cedar, 6' tall by 3' wide, 2001. The artist says that this piece is one of her personal favorites. "This piece is about romance—the male sun, in love with the female moon. Below them their child, Earth, and everything on it, looks up to their parents in the sky." Photo courtesy Bill Bailey.

▶ *Crooked Spine.* Western red cedar, 2' tall by 2' wide, 1997. Jessie enjoys carving the inner structure of objects — "the architecture of the temple."

▼ Jessie's *Tribute to Van Gogh* at Little Joe's Reno Contest, held at the Hilton in 2001. Salvaged ancient-growth coastal redwood, 6' tall by 8' wide. "Van Gogh must have had a lot of fun painting because it was a joy carving in his style."

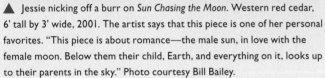

▲ Jessie carving *Broken Seashell* at the West Coast, The Big One! Sitka spruce, 7' tall by 3' wide. 1999. Photo by Rick Carver. "In life, sometimes you can feel broken, but even then it's still beautiful. And maybe you need to break the shell of your identity to see what is real inside." With this piece, Jessie became the first woman to place in the top 10 of The Big One!'s Judges' Choice category.

◀ *Flora.* A commissioned work in English holly, 14' tall by 1½' wide, 2003. "The height of the tree was no problem; the challenge was to get all of the images in there and make them seem proportional in a tree that was skinny and tall. I decided to carve the holly leaves as a homage to the tree."

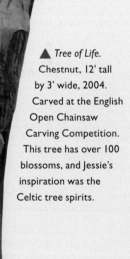

▲ *Tree of Life.* Chestnut, 12' tall by 3' wide, 2004. Carved at the English Open Chainsaw Carving Competition. This tree has over 100 blossoms, and Jessie's inspiration was the Celtic tree spirits.

A Note from the Author

My call to wood happened when I was a student at Western Washington University in Bellingham, Washington. A friend of mine mentioned a furniture-making class and almost immediately, I knew that working with wood was what I wanted to do with my life. Shortly after that revelation, I returned to my home, Whidbey Island, Washington. There, perhaps serendipitously, I met chainsaw sculptor Pat McVay and my journey on the chainsaw carving road began.

For six years, I immersed myself in the world of wood. I studied it, worked with it, and wrote about it. It was during this time that I first joined the Cascade Chainsaw Sculptors Guild. After a few years, I decided to take on the task of starting their newsletter, *The Cutting Edge*. At that time, there was simply no news available about the emerging art form of chainsaw carving, and it was my vision to document the work and events that were taking place for the future. Though I viewed the chainsaw carvers I met as true artists, it seemed that the general public did not recognize chainsaw carvers as artists. I hoped that, through my writing, I could help the art form gain the respect it deserved. The first newsletter was mailed to only ten people in May 1993. Even though readership was small, I kept at it because I loved meeting new artists, hearing their stories, and sharing them with others.

After six beautiful years of writing and working with wood, I decided to expand my artistic horizons beyond wood. I visited museums in the United States and Europe and immersed myself in the masters of art, such as Van Gogh, Rodin, El Greco, and Michelangelo. At the end of my self-guided study through the stone and bronze statues of yesterday, I realized that I longed for the great masterpieces of artists who were alive today. I continued my travels, this time seeking out chainsaw artists everywhere I went. The stories I collected were published in *The Cutting Edge*, which was soon being sent to hundreds of members.

After several years of gathering stories, I knew I wanted to put this book together as a homage to the wonderful people who have dedicated their lives to creating chainsaw wood sculpture. They are beautiful, spirited individuals, and their art form has it all—drama, excitement, speed, energy, and wood.

I hope you will enjoy reading these stories and learning about chainsaw carving as much as I have.

— *Jessie Groeschen*

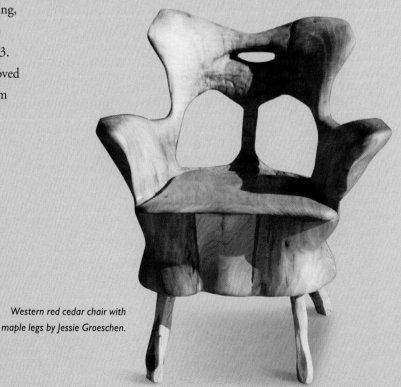

Western red cedar chair with maple legs by Jessie Groeschen.

Introduction

Speed, danger, and excitement are just three of the intriguing elements of chainsaw carving. Since 1980, this innovative method of woodcarving has gained momentum and has captured the attention of a growing number of artists and fans. Over the past three decades, an increasing number of competitions and chainsaw performances have attracted large crowds both nationally and internationally and have helped to promote chainsaw carving as an emerging art form. The danger involved in using a chainsaw, the dexterity and high level of skill required of the artist, and the raw beauty of the natural wood puts chainsaw carving in a class by itself.

This book is intended to be an insider's look at the major artists, both past and present, who have impacted the art form. Their work, methods, approaches, styles, backgrounds, and personalities are as varied as the grains on the multitude of wood they have carved. It is their uniqueness that makes this book, and the art form itself, so fascinating.

Chainsaw carving accommodates a tremendous variety of skill levels that include everything from rough-cut bears sold on the roadside to meticulously carved, museum-quality masterpieces sold only in galleries. Abilities range from carving a person's name on a belt buckle while he or she is wearing it to spending months fine-tuning a 20-foot wall mural to creating a two-story tree house large enough for adults to inhabit to creating a breathtaking soaring eagle during a 45-minute performance show. All this is done with a chainsaw.

Chainsaw carvers come from all walks of life—from woodsmen and loggers to art students and PhDs—and their styles can be anything, from flamboyant chainsaw performers drawing crowds of hundreds to those who live and work in complete seclusion. There are those whose names are well known and respected in art circles and those who choose total anonymity. Some enter their carvings in all of the top competitions, taking home the highest awards, while others refuse to offer their art up to subjective judgment. Many artists turned their hobbies into highly successful businesses, selling pieces within all 50 states and around the globe, while a few choose to carve simply for the love of it, not caring if they ever sell a single piece.

If you can think it, they can carve it. Styles run the gamut from lifelike to whimsical, from realistic to abstract, and from mythical to magical. Experience ranges from those completing a few hundred carvings to one artist who has carved over 51,000 pieces so far. Their works range in height from a delicate one-inch hummingbird to a whopping 35-foot totem pole and range in form from the pencil-thin legs of a heron to the thick, muscular power of a grizzly bear.

The availability of newer, faster, lightweight chainsaws that allowed for greater maneuverability and flexibility helped to propel chainsaw carving as an art form. These saws did little, however, to minimize the risk of injury and permanent damage to the carvers. In fact, chainsaw carvers suffer many ailments, such as permanent hearing loss, back problems, and nerve damage in the hands, shoulders, arms, and fingers.

Then, there are the violent, bloody injuries that require hundreds of stitches and may even result in the loss of limbs, ears, and fingers. The scars of their trade permanently mar many chainsaw carvers. Still, despite all the dangers posed by this art form, the lure of the chainsaw more than outweighs the fear.

This is the story of those fearless men and women whose pioneering efforts carved out a new art form for all to enjoy.

The History and Evolution of Chainsaw Carving

C hainsaw carving is an exciting development in the ancient tradition of woodcarving, an art form almost as old as man himself. Woodcarving began out of necessity, as early man fashioned primitive tools by shaping wood with sharp rocks and bones. As man's technology improved and new carving tools developed, woodcarving for function and art began to appear.

Objects carved from wood were frequently used for religious purposes, especially by the Egyptians. Early statues of their gods and goddesses were carved in wood. However, woodcarving did not receive its real development until over 2,000 years ago, when tools and methods for carving became more refined. Because of the perishable character of wood, it is easy to understand why only a small number of the woodcarvings from antiquity still exist today.

Throughout the ages, woodcarving continued to develop, as did its tools—saws, axes, knives, mallets, and awls. But a real advancement, as far as chainsaw carving goes, did not occur until 1830. At that time, a new type of instrument hit the scene, although it was originally intended for quite a different purpose.

Early chainsaws

The osteotome was an orthopedic surgical tool invented in 1830 by the German prosthetics maker, Bernard Heine. It was developed as an easier means of cutting through bone—an alternative to using a hammer or a chisel or a reciprocating saw. Turning the handle of a sprocket wheel moved a chain around a guiding blade, thus creating the first chain saw. The links of the chain carried small, angled cutting teeth.

For woodcutting purposes, it is purported that a California inventor named R.L. Muir may have been the first to put blades on a chain. However, this machine weighed hundreds of pounds and was never a commercial success.

One of the earliest chainsaw carvers, Mike McVay (left), poses with the Timber Festival Queen and a friend at the Albany Timber Festival held in Albany, Oregon. A 30' portrait of Paul Bunyan stands in the background.

Other early chainsaw-type tools included the Hamilton saw of 1861 that was hand-cranked and looked like a spinning wheel, and the American Riding Machine, which appeared in the 1880s and looked like a rowing machine with blades on it.

Timberman Magazine reports that the first experiment with a gasoline chainsaw may have been during the summer of 1905 in Eureka, California. Powered by a two-cylinder, water-cooled motor set at 90 degrees from its normal position, it sawed through a ten-foot log in 4.5 minutes.

The first modern chainsaw

The accomplishments of the early chainsaw inventors paved the way for a German mechanical engineer named Andreas Stihl, who is believed to be the inventor of the modern chainsaw. In 1926, he designed the first bucking chainsaw with an electric motor. This was publicly accepted as the first "real" chainsaw. It was also the first mobile chainsaw. In 1929, he also patented the first petrol-driven chainsaw, which was operated by two men and known as "the tree-felling machine." These patents were the first successful ones for hand-held mobile chainsaws designed for cutting wood.

In 1938, Stihl designed a two-man, petrol-driven chainsaw. This was followed in 1950 by what is claimed by the company to be the world's first petrol-driven chainsaw for a single operator. Weighing just over 35 pounds, it was equipped with a manually adjusted swivel carburetor that allowed the saw to be used not only for bucking, but also for felling.

McCulloch, Pioneer, and other companies soon followed suit, and the race was on for lighter, faster, and more powerful chainsaws. With those early, relatively lightweight chainsaws came increased maneuverability—enough so that some people began to experiment and discover other creative uses for the chainsaw.

Chain

In autumn of 1946, logger/inventor Joseph Buford Cox was chopping firewood when he noticed a timber beetle larva, about the size of a nickel, easily chomping its way through the wood, going both across and with the grain.

As an experienced operator of the gas-powered saws used in those days, Cox knew what a problem the cutting chain could be, requiring a lot of filing and maintenance. He suspected that if he could just duplicate that larva's alternating C-shaped jaws in steel, he could make a better chain.

Working in the basement shop of his home in Portland, Oregon, Cox devised a revolutionary new chain. The first Cox Chipper Chain was produced and sold in November 1947. Many chainsaw manufacturers still use a version of that original chain today.

Vintage chainsaws can be appreciated as art themselves.

Bars

Another revolutionary moment in chainsaw carving history was the invention of the carving bar. Designed specifically for carving, the tiny tip allows a person to bore into the wood with little or no kickback. Noted chainsaw carver Don Colp claims to have had an idea about a narrower-tipped bar: he passed this information to Windsor Bar, and the quarter-tip carving bar was born. Mike McVay, another early chainsaw carver, claims to have coined the phrase for the different sizes—dime tip and quarter tip—by putting a coin on the end of these new bars, and this terminology is still used today.

Pioneers—the first chainsaw artists

Unlike with the development of the chainsaw itself, there are no records of who actually may have created the very first chainsaw carving—only oral histories of what others may have seen and heard. There is really no way of knowing who in what part of the world might have picked up the chainsaw and carved a piece of art for the very first time.

However, in this book, you will read about the earliest recognized pioneers—chainsaw carvers, such as "Wild Mountain Man" Ray Murphy and Ken Kaiser, whose early chainsaw artwork dates back to the 1950s.

In 1953, a young Ray Murphy used his dad's chainsaw to spell out his brother's name in a piece of wood. Later in life, he would travel and demonstrate this same type of work, carving names on wooden belt buckles worn by his customers.

In 1961, Ken Kaiser created the Trail of Tall Tales, commissioned by the Trees of Mystery, a tourist attraction in Northern

California. He carved 50 monumental pieces, which focused on Paul Bunyan, in gigantic redwood logs and panels.

The formative years

During the 1960s and 1970s, more and more people began to experiment with chainsaw carving. These years saw the work of a number of chainsaw carvers, including Lois Hollingsworth, Mike McVay, Susan Miller, Don Colp, Judy McVay, and Brenda Hubbard. Some had already discovered their artistic talent and viewed the chainsaw as another untapped resource; others picked up the chainsaw and for the first time discovered an artistic talent in themselves that they never knew they had. The cord that bound them all together was a deep love of wood and their ability to master a chainsaw.

By the dawn of the 1980s, the art of chainsaw carving became a bit more established with the book *Fun and Profitable Chainsaw Carving* by William Westenhaver and Ronald Hovde circulating.

Traveling chainsaw carvers loaded their carvings in the backs of their trucks, which served as traveling galleries. Chainsaw carving shops sprang up on the roadside, catching some of the local traffic. Chainsaw carving as performance art also became popular at county and state fairs and malls across America. And thanks to the competitive forces of chainsaw companies, chainsaw carving contests started cropping up as well.

In the 1990s, chainsaw carving evolved even further and was developed and promoted as an art form, receiving more acceptance and more public recognition. Carving contests became more prevalent across the country with the backing of saw companies, who started to support contests financially around the turn of the 21st century.

The art form today

Today, chainsaw carving encompasses a wide variety of styles, skill levels, and themes. Some artists are strictly performance artists who draw large audiences and are interested in pieces that can be done quickly. Others work for months on one piece, perfecting the sculpture for display in an art gallery. Themes involve anything imaginable, from wildlife to figures to tree houses. Chainsaw carving shows, too, have increased

in number to reflect the growing art form. And there are numerous classes available to teach the techniques of carving with a chainsaw.

Included in this book are some early and contemporary chainsaw artists from many of the different carving styles. There are also profiles of some of the top shows as well as the people responsible for bringing them to life.

The power of a master woodcarver lies in the skills and techniques he or she has acquired—filing, sharpening, and understanding his or her tools and timber. The power of a good artist is in his or her imagination. As Einstein said, "Imagination is greater than knowledge." A successful chainsaw carver must have them both.

This redwood mural by Ken Kaiser—one of the earliest recognized pioneers—still stands at the Trees of Mystery in Northern California.

➤ Part One ◄

The Early Artists

While we cannot pinpoint who may have created the very first chainsaw carving, we can, however, look at the work of some of the earliest pioneers, some of whom were carving as far back as the 1950s. With the work of these artists, we see the beginnings of a number of different styles of chainsaw carving, including stunt/entertainment carving, sculptures, murals, and abstract forms. Each of the artists featured in this section created his or her own unique style and, in doing so, rough-shaped the world of chainsaw art.

Ray Murphy

HANCOCK, MAINE

A journey down the road of chainsaw art inevitably winds its way back to Ray Murphy, otherwise known as the "Wild Mountain Man." His exploits with a chainsaw go back as far as 1953, to what he claims was the world's first piece of chainsaw art. Since then he has carved nearly 51,000 pieces of art—everything from a 35-foot totem pole to a two-inch turtle. His work can be found in all 50 states and across all seven continents.

Known for his wild and innovative chainsaw art techniques, Ray stunned the public with many daring feats. His work is displayed in Ripley's Believe It or Not! Museums around the world and has been featured in books, television programs, and more than 8,000 newspaper and magazine articles.

He may also hold the world record for the most injuries to a chainsaw artist, with 33 serious mishaps resulting in hundreds of stitches. Even though he lost two fingers on his right hand in one such accident, Ray claims that the injury in 1977 was his worst.

"I was cutting a tree when the saw got caught and kicked back into my face. It just got away from me. I thought I had cut my ear off; instead it cut right down the side of my face. Blood was spurting everywhere, and the guy working next to me nearly fainted. I had no idea how bad it was at first because when a chainsaw cuts, it lays the skin back over. It took 50-something stitches to close it up. That's why I wear a beard—to hide that scar," he tells us.

▲ Ray shows off one of his smaller pieces, a tiny ladybug carved with a chainsaw only. Later he added paint. "I prefer my pieces natural, but some things need to be painted—like a skunk, for example, has to be black and white, while a fisherman from Maine needs a bright yellow slicker. So I paint these pieces to add realism."

◀ A focal point in Ray's studio is this stunning seven-foot-tall angel, which bears the face of his wife, Emilina.

Journal

Many thoughts were running through my head as I went to meet the guru of entertainment and stunt-style chainsaw art—the Wild Mountain Man, a.k.a. Ray Murphy. I wondered...how wild is he? I had heard many stories from other carvers about his wild and innovative chainsaw art techniques, but I realized I had never heard anything wild about his manners.

I drove from Washington State, the northwest corner of the United States, to the northeast corner, the state of Maine. The trip took me 3,000 miles over 5 days—a somewhat fitting homage to the man who put over a million miles on his Greyhound bus, driving around America to perform his traveling chainsaw art road show.

Suddenly, there I was at his shop. I introduced myself, and he gave me a great big hug. Meeting Ray was like finding an old, lost friend.

—Jessie

▲ A wall inside Ray's workshop is devoted entirely to displaying his fine, feathered friends. Each bird is rich in detail and finely painted. "To be able to put round eyeballs in a tiny bird's head 100 percent by chainsaw is something that amazes even me," says Ray.

"Whenever a person gets hurt with a chainsaw, there are usually three factors: fatigue, overconfidence, and distraction. Getting hurt like that makes you humble. You learn to really respect that machine."

One of twelve children, Ray was raised on the Wind River Reservation in Wyoming (his mother was Shoshone), where he learned early on that life was tough and making a living difficult. By the tender age of ten, he and his brother supplemented the family income by cutting up firewood.

"My brother and I were using an old crosscut saw to cut the wood, but we needed to do it faster than we could with that old 'misery whip.'- We knew we weren't supposed to go into my dad's workshop and use his chainsaw, but we did anyway. Afterwards we cleaned everything up real good and put it all away exactly the way it was. We figured that we'd gotten away with it. But, in the end, the sawdust gave us away, and we got a good whooping."

Not much later, his father taught him the proper methods of handling a chainsaw, and Ray grew quite proficient. When the straight-A student wasn't cutting wood, he'd be playing around carving messages into logs for his brother to read. In 1953, at only eleven years of age, he created what he thinks was the world's first chainsaw art by sawing designs into logs and faces into fence posts. By 1960, the teenager had sold his first sculpture.

"I was making some furniture at the time when I started playing around with the chainsaw. It was the kind with the old scratcher chain that would jump up and down and kick and bounce. I was having a good old time when suddenly an idea just popped into my head, and I started cutting 'wind faces' on the arms of a bench I working on. I was so amazed at how they turned out. I just couldn't believe it," says the guru of entertainment/stunt chainsaw art.

"Even today I surprise myself, thinking 'how on earth did I do that?'—especially the eyes in my sculptures. To be able to put round eyeballs in a tiny bird's head 100 percent by chainsaw is something that amazes even me."

▶ Here is a peek inside Ray's historic bus/museum, where the artist shows off one of his vintage chainsaws.

Ray Murphy

The following text appears on the sign in the photograph:

WILD MOUNTAIN MAN · The Living Legend
ORIGINATED THE ART OF SCULPTURING WITH CHAIN SAW
FEATURED ... RADIO & MAGAZINES & OVER 8000 NEWSP...
SET ... WON AT MANY NATIONAL + WORLD CHAMP...
WROTE ... ABET... 79 · WORLD'S FIRST STAGE SHOW
ONLY PE... ON TO SCULPT WITH TWO SAWS AT SAME TIME 1980
PUBLIS... O W... WHILE ... RIPLEY'S BELIEVE IT OR NO...
EAGLE N WHITE ... 1982 ,88 · WROTE NAME ON BELT BU...
DUBBED BY ... ORLD'S FOREMOST TRICK ARTIST WITH C... AW
COMPLETED WORK N... O ATES 1985 · ALL 7 CONTINENTS
OR... S... WOMO... TV COMME...

▲ The Wild Mountain Man's bus/museum. During a 25-year period of traveling the countryside, Ray traveled over 1,000,000 miles in this bus, thrilling the public with his one-man chainsaw carving show.

What happened to that famed bench? "I actually sold it to my bus driver," he laughs.

After high school, Ray went on to eventually earn two college degrees, one in forestry and the other in structural engineering. The self-taught artist says his art is a culmination of all of his life experiences.

"As a kid, I couldn't sketch a thing. I never even considered doing artwork, although I always admired those who could. So I never had any formal art training. Many people have said I should go and learn—that it might improve my work. But why should I learn to do somebody else's work? Let them copy me!"

And copy him they have. Many other artists have incorporated his two-chainsaw stunt into their acts, and the bunny carving, so popular with lumberjack shows, originated with him. Even when his fame spread across the globe, Ray managed to maintain a healthy outlook.

"The problem with fame is that you spend half your time posing for photographs," he chuckles. "I got a wall full of trophies—big deal. They're all just dust collectors. The main thing is having fun. I'm having a ball."

But life wasn't all fun and games for this mountain man. For years, Ray struggled with alcoholism. His stories are all too familiar and very sobering.

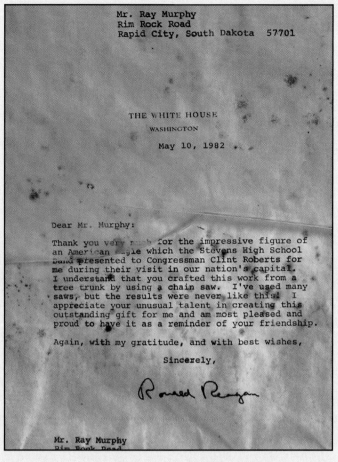

Mr. Ray Murphy
Rim Rock Road
Rapid City, South Dakota   57701

THE WHITE HOUSE

WASHINGTON

May 10, 1982

Dear Mr. Murphy:

Thank you very much for the impressive figure of
an American eagle which the Stevens High School
Band presented to Congressman Clint Roberts for
me during their visit in our nation's capital.
I understand that you crafted this work from a
tree trunk by using a chain saw. I've used many
saws, but the results were never like this! I
appreciate your unusual talent in creating this
outstanding gift for me and am most pleased and
proud to have it as a reminder of your friendship.

Again, with my gratitude, and with best wishes,

Sincerely,

Ronald Reagan

Mr. Ray Murphy
Rim Rock Road

▲ A letter from President Reagan thanking Ray for one of his
chainsaw art pieces and praising him for his unusual talent.

▶ A timeline, proudly displayed outside the artist's studio, highlights some
of his major accomplishments. "I've done so many things in my lifetime
that it's hard for me to keep track of them all," laughs Ray.

Wild Mountain Man

1952 STARTED USING CHAINSAWS - AGE 10
1953 MADE WORLD'S FIRST CHAINSAW ART
1954 CUT+SOLD FIREWOOD+FENCE POST
1960 SOLD FIRST SCULPTURE
1962-65 TRAVELED U.S.+CANADA LOGGING
1966-70 WENT TO COLLEGE-CWC+U.WYO.
1971-1973 GOT JOURNEYMAN IRONWORKERS BOOK
1974-79 COMPETED IN LUMBERJACK COMPETITIONS
1976 SET THREE WORLD RECORDS
1979 SAWED ALPHABET ON PENCIL FIRST TIME
1980 DID WORLD'S FIRST SAW SCULPTURE STAGE SHOW
1981 FEATURED IN "RIPLEY'S BELIEVE IT OR NOT"
1982 ON A.B.C. WIDE WORLD OF SPORTS
1983 WON ALL NATIONAL+WORLD CHAMPIONSHIPS
1985-87 COMPLETED WORK 50 STATES-7 CONTINENTS
1988 JUNE 2 NEW WORLD RECORD CHAIR = 10 SECONDS
1995 BECOME "COLLECTABLE"-OLD FARMERS ALMANAC
1999 BEARS ON FRONT COVER "GREAT AMERICAN ROAD TRIP"
2000 FILMED SAWING 10 NUMBERS ON TOOTHPICK-RIPLEY'S
2002 FEATURED IN TIM SAMPLE'S BOOK "MAINE" Curiosities
2003 July 28: 50,000 PEICES MADE + 50 YEARS

◀ These are a few of the famed
pencils upon which Ray carved
the entire English alphabet.
This stunt earned him a place in
the annals of Ripley's Believe It
or Not! in 1979. One of these
pencils is now on display at every
Ripley's Museum worldwide.

Ray Murphy

▲ Ray performs his carving-a-name-in-a-wooden-belt-buckle stunt on this brave young woman—a feat he has accomplished without injury nearly 10,000 times. "It's good to get someone with a firm stomach, calm nerves, and a short name!" Photo by Pat McVay.

▲ Wild Man Murphy's love of wildlife is evidenced by his amazing array of animal and bird carvings. These lively, life-size bunnies—typical of Ray's show bunnies—were hand painted for a more warm and fuzzy appearance.

"My life started in January of 1978 when I finally got sober," Ray attests. "I wanted to quit drinking because I wanted to do this artwork so bad, and I knew that, at the rate I was going, it just wasn't going to happen."

The amazing Wild Mountain Man

A string of stunning firsts evidenced his turnaround, starting in 1979 when he amazed the world by sawing the alphabet on a #2 pencil. "More and more people were coming into chainsaw carving with all their fancy equipment, and I knew I had to separate myself from everybody else in the world. That pencil was the first step. I now have one of those pencils in every Ripley's Believe It or Not! Museum worldwide."

In St. Louis in 1980, he performed his first stage show. For the next five years, he toured the country thrilling showgoers with stunts like that. He put more than a million miles on his converted Greyhound bus/museum, which became a familiar sight at shows, fairs, rodeos, logging competitions, and other events.

In 1981, he stunned a crowd by sawing his name into a belt buckle worn by his son. Then he stunned himself.

"My son had been wearing a pad under his shirt with a metal plate over it for this demonstration. About the eighth day of the show he said, 'Dad, do I really have to wear that stuff? It's so uncomfortable, and it's really not necessary. I haven't worn it for the past three shows.' I was so shocked! I couldn't believe he had done that," he quips. Since then, Ray has sawn over 10,000 belt buckles on unprotected bellies. "I even did one for Miss North Carolina who wore a belt buckle in a bikini!"

Ray introduced another thriller in 1983—using two chainsaws at a time to work on a sculpture. This was something never before attempted, and it quickly became a show pleaser. As other chainsaw carvers scrambled to duplicate the act, Ray did them one better. This next incredible feat became his fourth entry in Ripley's annals—using two chainsaws to simultaneously saw two separate and different sculptures.

"I've had psychologists want to study me to see how I did that," he chuckles. But to Ray the explanation is simple. "I'm right-handed, so, when I lost the two fingers on my right hand, I had to learn to do a lot of things with my left hand.

And what happened was I became very proficient and accurate with my left hand. I even learned to sketch as good with my left as with my right."

In 1988, a woman at one of Ray's shows turned her head for just a moment and missed the entire act. That's because Ray had managed the feat of chainsawing a chair in ten seconds flat! That became his fifth world record.

Next on his list of firsts was carving his name on the head of a match. It was in direct response to another artist's challenge. "I had someone tell me about another carver who had carved a name on a matchstick, adding that my pencil trick was no longer a big deal. So I wrote my name on the head of a match without striking it and sent it back to the guy!"

In 2000, Ray performed a feat that had taken years to perfect—one that is spoken of in a kind of reverence by other chainsaw carvers. It is the ultimate act with a chainsaw: writing ten numbers on a toothpick.

"Doing ten numbers on a toothpick is so close to impossible that I doubt that there will ever be another person who can duplicate that," insists Ray. "Here is where all of these life experiences come into play: structural engineering, angles, lighting, mechanics, concentration, and even martial arts because you have to have controlled breathing in order to make your body stay perfectly still. Mathematically, everything has to be exactly right for this thing to work. The movement of the saw and arm is done by letting in or out a breath and is so slight that it can't be seen."

Lighting is critical too, says the artist. It has to be absolutely perfect so as not to cast any shadows. Some days it takes longer than others, but Ray can usually accomplish this seemingly impossible feat in around three minutes' time.

"You learn a lot about yourself when you're doing this kind of thing. It's mind over matter and having my body completely in tune with the chainsaw. And it's mental discipline. But before you get any good music, you have to practice."

Today Ray lives and works in a rural area of upstate Maine, about 90 miles from the Canadian border. He spends time working with the D.A.R.E. program, traveling the school circuit speaking to children about the pitfalls of alcohol. He also serves as a mentor to other artists, taking many under his wing. "To be an artist, and to be successful, you cannot be greedy. You have to share. God gave you that talent to share, not to hoard."

Never even entertaining a thought of retirement, the 62-year-old chainsaw artist is now preparing for his next big show, right in his own backyard.

"What I've got here is a 60' by 80' steel building with a stage and a bleacher system. In between them is hockey glass, which will serve to protect the public and shield the noise. I've got an entire 90-minute show I'm working on that incorporates many of my record-breaking acts, including ten numbers on a toothpick," he explains.

Even though they may not believe their eyes, all are welcome to come and watch the show, which he feels will elevate the art of chainsaw carving to new and greater heights. With so many highlights in such a long, successful career, Ray says it's hard to pick a favorite.

"There are just so darn many things that have happened in my life that it's hard to keep track of them all. I never imagined I'd ever be doing what I'm doing now. This has gone way beyond my wildest dreams."

▲ Wild Mountain Man during a chainsaw demonstration. "I am not a carver, I am a sawyer," he insists.

BOOT`EM

Kenyon Kaiser

MONTANA

Ken Kaiser dreamt of becoming an artist ever since his youth growing up in Montana. But after graduating from the Montana State University, he chose the practical road, settling instead to operate a chain of music stores. Still, the urge to study art persisted. Finally giving in, he entered the University of Oregon as an art major while continuing to run the piano business.

It was almost by accident that he discovered the chainsaw and immediately realized it was suited to his talents. But Ken Kaiser had no mentor, for he was exploring uncharted waters.

Susan Miller, who took up chainsaw carving in the mid-60s, was a student at the University of Oregon not long after Ken had graduated. She recalls the reactions of the faculty to his radical art form.

"Sadly his work was not taken seriously by the art department because of his choice of sculpture tool. They just could not accept the chainsaw as a means of creating art back then."

In 1959, Ken gave up his thriving piano business to tour Oregon as a representative for a chainsaw distributor, exhibiting his chainsaw art at events such as the Portland Rose Festival. It was just a year and a half later that he was commissioned to carve his name in history.

Making his mark

Deep in the heart of The Redwood National and State Parks lies a little tourist attraction called "Trees of Mystery" located in Klamath, California. Nestled under the looming giants on California's north coast, this fascinating nature attraction has welcomed visitors for over 50 years. It features one of the largest privately owned Native American museums as well unusual redwood tree formations and a sky rail ride through

▲ Ken Kaiser stands beside a wood bust that he carved of his wife.

Journal

I heard about Ken Kaiser when I was working on a statue for a place called the Saw Blade, which used to be a logger bar and family restaurant. The local people said that Ken used to frequent the Saw Blade back in his day.

After marveling over Ken's art on the Trail of Tall Tales, I felt that the man was inspired in a great way—by the wood, the forests, the people—and he had let it all out. Unfortunately, I will never meet the man who spent ten months carving 50 large redwood pieces in the heart of a beautiful forest. Fortunately for us, his art is still here.

—Jessie

◄ Nestled in a fern setting is Boot 'Em, standing 7' in height and 8' in width.

▲ Four faces on the trail. From left to right: *Choker Charlie*, *Time Tony*, *Short Haul Hanson*, and *Dull of the Woods*. The piece is 7' high by 16' long.

▲ Trees of Mystery in Klamath, California, is located directly in the center of the Redwood National and State Parks in northern California.

▲ A post along the trail.

▲ *Cookey—World's Fastest Waiter* is 10' high and 4' wide.

the redwoods. But by far its biggest draw is the world's largest collection of Ken Kaiser chainsaw carvings.

A pioneer in the area of chainsaw art, many believe Ken Kaiser's carved murals belong in a museum, but what better museum to showcase his chainsaw art than in this forest setting where the world's greatest trees grow?

Averaging 8 feet to as much as 20 feet in diameter with some as tall as 375 feet (taller than the Statue of Liberty from the base of the pedestal to the tip of the torch), these giant redwoods are absolutely the largest living things on earth.

Guarding the entrance to the Trees of Mystery is a 49-foot statue of the fabled logger Paul Bunyan and his gigantic blue ox, Babe. To keep the legends of this logger alive, the owners hoped to portray his antics amongst the redwoods.

"The Seattle World's Fair was coming up in 1962, and my parents were looking to make a number of vast improvements to the Trees of Mystery. One of the concepts they came up with was to have a section on our tour that depicts the tales of Paul Bunyan in redwood carvings done by a chainsaw. Back in those days, there were only about five people in the world who knew how to do that because it was a brand-new art form," says John Thompson, manager of the family-owned business. "They had seen Ken carving somewhere up in Oregon and commissioned him to do the work."

The legends of Paul Bunyan, the greatest logger who ever lived, are a compilation of tall tales that were started by lumberjacks sitting around a bunkhouse stove.

"Like with any American folklore, you have to keep making up new tall tales to keep the legend alive. So my mother, Marylee Thompson, created new 'tall tales' for Ken to carve. My father, Ray Thompson, procured the largest pieces of milled redwood in the world for this project."

In 1961, armed with Marylee Thompson's enchanting stories, a chainsaw, the world's largest redwood panels, and a Paul-Bunyan-sized imagination, Ken Kaiser created the 50-plus sculptures and carved murals seen on the Trail of Tall Tales. The project took six months to complete and stands as a monument to his life.

▲ This redwood mural titled *The Bunk House* is 7' in height and 12' in width.

▼ A broader look at beautifully detailed redwood murals on the Trail of Tall Tales, depicting the yarns of Paul Bunyan and his cronies.

► This redwood mural, *Babe Is Found*, is 7' high by 8' wide.

▲ *Paul's Book Larnin'*, 7' high by 4' wide.

▲ A note to Paul Bunyan's girlfriend. Notice all of the carved names and initials made over the years by visitors on the trail. The piece is 7' high by 4' wide.

◄ *Paul Bunyan's Girlfriend* is beautifully depicted in this 8' high by 8' wide by 6' deep carving. Photo courtesy Trees of Mystery.

▼ *Paul Bunyan and the Big Fish* is 7' high by 8' wide.

Mike McVay

WHIDBEY ISLAND, WASHINGTON
WASILLA, ALASKA

Always curious, always testing himself, and never afraid to try something new, it's no surprise that Mike McVay eventually picked up the chainsaw as a carving tool. It was his father who first gave him the idea. Every summer during the 1950s and early 1960s, Mike worked for his father's salvage diving company in Oregon. "At Eel Lake, we had a big burn pile for huge stumps, usually 6' to 8' tall, that were being removed from the lake. I was using an ax and chopping faces into the stumps prior to them being burned. It was a lot of work with the ax, so my dad suggested using a chainsaw along with the ax. Mostly, I think he wanted me to get back to work. And that's how it all began," Mike recalls.

However, Mike's interest in wood began much earlier. He began whittling at age eight, when his mother gave him his first pocketknife—a gift meant to steer him away from beating his drum. "Somebody else had given me a drum for my birthday. After a few days, my mother gave me the knife and asked, 'What's inside that drum that makes all that noise?'" Ever curious, Mike took the pocketknife and cut right into the drum to see what was inside. "After that, I became a woodcarver," he laughs.

By the early 1960s, Mike began attending arts and crafts fairs, selling his line of small animals and decorative artwork. "In those days, it was hard to sell stuff because nobody was sure that they were buying anything of value. Today, there's no reason that a woodcarver should go hungry," Mike says.

During this time, Mike also started a production carving shop, which turned into a thriving business, shipping carvings around the world. He also traveled around the country, educating carvers and planting the seeds of the art form. "I would go to a place, do a demonstration, and come back the next year to find three more carvers. I felt like Johnny Appleseed."

▲ Mike McVay and his *Gunslinger* in 1985. Photo courtesy Mike McVay.

Journal

I met Mike McVay in 1993 after I had started The Cutting Edge newsletter with Pat McVay, who mentioned that his brother had carved for the 1964 New York World's Fair. It sounded incredible, so I asked Pat's brother, Mike, if I could write a story about him for our newsletter. Mike happily agreed and gave me an entertaining story. That was when I learned of Ken Kaiser's influence on Mike's art. I had also heard that he used to do public readings of E. E. Cummings' poetry. I am also a fan of Cummings, so I asked Mike if the rumors were true. Off the top of his head, he recited Cummings' poem "Buffalo Bill." Whether he was rattling off poetry or sharing his knowledge of the chainsaw and woodcarving, he always left me thoroughly impressed.

—Jessie

◄ *Viking Mascot* in Healy, Alaska. Photo by Mike McVay.

"I think I was the first person to sharpen a pencil with a chainsaw in the 1960s, while I was in Indiana. It was almost a week-long show, and they were giving out carpenter's pencils at the fair. So, a guy came up to me and said, 'You're pretty good with that saw. Can you sharpen this pencil?' I said, 'I'll do it if you'll hold it.' And he held it steady, away from his body, and I sharpened up both sides. He just walked away shaking his head."

As Mike continued to perform the stunt, he started using the biggest saw that he could find. "Saws back then were scary things. When I'd get ready to sharpen the pencil, women would cover their eyes. The men would get all glassy-eyed, hoping that no accidents would happen and partially hoping that an accident would happen."

In 1962, Mike met Ken Kaiser at the Trees of Mystery. "My father and I drove to northern California to meet Ken because we heard that he was doing amazing work. He had been going up and down the coast carving heads of figures like Abraham Lincoln."

"Ken was using big saws, but, about that time, smaller models started to appear on the market. There was no vibration dampening at all. Your fingers were numb by the end of a workday. And those were the best saws of the day."

Mike met up with Ken again in 1964 at the New York World's Fair, where both men were asked to carve. Mark Hatfield, the governor of Oregon, had invited Mike to attend. "I got a job carving 110 feet of murals for the front of the Oregon building at the World's Fair. Going to New York was amazing for a country boy like me. We had a lot of good experiences." Mike also attended the 1965 World's Fair, where he carved totem poles of the 50 states for the Boy Scouts of America.

When his production shop was lost in a fire in 1966, Mike moved to Saudi Arabia to work for his father's diving company. A year later, he ended up in Paris, France. There, he taught English and dabbled in acting, writing, and directing. Mike also made furniture and chainsaw carved to get by. What really affected him was the amount of artwork that was accessible everyday but taken for granted by most people. "Paris was incredible. I remember stepping out of the subway and seeing Rodin's *Balzac*. It was in an early morning drizzle, and he

[the statue] was standing there, pulling his robes around him against the chill, looking disgusted, impervious to the pigeons, about to step off to his right and head down the Boulevard Montparnasse where he might find a comfortable seat in a warm café. And nobody else seemed to notice," Mike says.

Being constantly surrounded by artwork also had an effect on Mike's carving. "It was inspirational and overwhelming all at once. Especially after having seen only those boring little pictures in art history books. The size of the real thing was so awesome, the scale so huge, the emotional reaction so visceral. I wondered, 'Why would I ever want to carve little things?'" The experience helped to solidify Mike's interest in larger works of chainsaw art.

Around 1973, Mike returned to the U.S. permanently and started another carving business, this time with his sister Judy and his brother, Pat. The trio did a variety of carvings. Most memorable were the ones that showed off each of their particular talents. Mike especially remembers a 20-foot-tall rain gauge that they did for the Quinault Lodge, where the average rainfall is 17 feet. "We put it up on July 3, and there had already been nine feet of rain that year. It was carved with a sun raven at the top, trying to poke his head through the clouds. It was metered off every six inches with a crossbar that ran up and down, according to the rainfall. Judy painted it so that the colors went from very dark blue to symbol- ize the coldest rain with lots of green shades to symbolize vegetation, up through the color chart so it topped out in the brightest yellow to symbolize the sun." Though the family business didn't work out, Mike remained in Washington and continued to carve.

After a few years, Mike's restlessness and curiosity struck again, and he moved to Alaska. "Everybody up there seemed to do anything they wanted to do. And they did it with so much gusto," Mike says. Because of the problems involved in carving frozen wood, Mike took on other jobs, like being a dog musher, in the winter. Finally, he set up shop in Alaska, spending his summers there and his winters in Washington. "I used to make a lot of carvings on speculation to see what

◀ Shown are five of the six panels about Oregon history that Mike carved for the New York World's Fair in 1964. The bottom right photo shows Mike with the Pioneer saw that he used to carve the panels. Photos courtesy Mike McVay.

This carving of a Kenai River king salmon is 56" long and is actually a weathervane. Mike's inspiration was a king salmon he caught that weighed 67 pounds. Photo by Mike McVay.

Mike and *Ostrich Hunter*, made of Sitka spruce.

These 20'-tall totem poles reside in Willow, Alaska. Photo by Mike McVay.

would sell, but now I do almost all commission. I found that by having a place alongside the road, I have all the business I can handle. Just be there—*be there*—and you'll be successful."

Though he says he is conscious of paying the bills, he does get to carve what he enjoys. "I enjoy doing wildlife, but I like doing caricatures as well."

Through all of his life experiences, Mike has remained a woodcarver. "At one point, I was trying to be a purist about the saw and use only the saw. But, I'm a woodcarver and not necessarily a chainsaw woodcarver. I started out with knives and gouges and bandages. I like the chainsaw because it allows me to carve without getting my fingers in the way. But I still use what gets the job done."

Carver, teacher

Mike McVay's contribution to chainsaw art includes more than just his carvings; it also includes the man himself. His teachings and influence stretch far and wide.

The first student Mike taught was Susan Miller. "Susan Miller showed up at my house one day, in the company of her aunt. She was recognizable immediately as a kindred spirit. She cast an aura that was palpable and, when I stepped into it, ostensibly to shake her hand, I was smitten. And, though we sometimes don't see each other for months—or even years—we have been friends forever. She was the first student to whom I had to explain what I did. I remember how difficult that was because I had always simply done it, never explaining." Mike says.

Mike also organized the first recorded chainsaw carving contest, the first World Championships in Puyallup, Washington, in 1981, an event that started the numerous shows and competitions that exist today. "I just wanted to get everybody together, and then it turned into a competition. I got the idea from a pool tournament. Here were all these people packed—jam-packed—competing for a ham!" And, competition raises the bar, allowing carvers to push themselves to their artistic limits.

"Picasso said, 'Every child is an artist and adults must rediscover it.' Isn't that what chainsaw carvers are doing? Some dorky hillbilly from

Pelican. The large number of pelicans that spend their summers along the Alaskan coast off the Bering Sea inspired this carving.

some remote area likes to whittle. The teacher says, 'Stop that, and pay attention to geography. You're never going to amount to anything if you keep that up!' It's a life headed down the wrong trail. Then he discovers the chainsaw and quickly learns he can make great big carvings. Carvings he can sell. Carvings for which people praise him and put his picture in the paper. He is acceptable. He fits in. Soon others come to see him. He shows them everything he can. They show others. Over time the unusual becomes better known, but it never becomes common," Mike says.

What advice would Mike have for chainsaw carvers or would-be chainsaw carvers today? That the chainsaw is about its speed and technology. "Power tools are the way to go. Why hand wash dishes if you have a dishwasher? The chainsaw is a good tool; it cuts wood. But the carver has to tell it what to do, to give it direction."

For Mike, much of his life's work stems from his desire to learn. "I've always been curious. And there's a lot I've done and a lot I haven't done. I am always testing myself," Mike says. And, his experiences have certainly shaped his philosophy in life and in woodcarving. "I love working with wood, and I like the temporal nature of the medium. Unlike bronze, it doesn't last forever. It's given me a better perspective on my own mortality and life expectations."

"Most of life's pleasures are short-lived, like a good meal or good friends. Some things last longer than others, but eventually they vanish and, hopefully, are replaced by others. I like discovering the spirit inside, releasing the form, enjoying the process. Once a piece is finished, I'm really not interested in it anymore. It's the next one that counts, that leads me on. Like that good meal, you can't eat it twice. It was satisfying at the time, maybe you learned a little something, but you have to move on."

Lois Hollingsworth

MIRANDA, CALIFORNIA

From flying a plane and driving a convoy truck for the U.S. Coast Guard during WWII to designing and building houses to living alone in the wild without electricity to quite possibly being the first woman to ever chainsaw carve, Lois Hollingsworth is a daring female pioneer who knows no bounds. No matter that her petite 5' 2" frame barely holds 100 pounds—if it was something she wanted to do, she found a way to do it.

Even today, the 80-year-old mother of two, grandmother of five, and great-grandmother of one thinks nothing of hiking through the remote woods that surround her isolated cabin. With chainsaw in tow, she hacks off hunks of wood and drags them back to her tool shed where she transforms them into beautiful works of art. One time, she was so moved by a piece of driftwood on the beach that she loaded it into her vehicle by herself and brought it home where it took four guys to move it. "Isn't adrenaline great!" she laughs.

"I've always done woodcarving, ever since I was a little kid and started carving sticks with a knife. It's just what I do. I've always been working in wood one way or another all of my life, carving with it or building with it," affirms Lois.

After high school, the native Californian earned an art degree from the University of California at Berkeley, where she was also breaking new ground. "I was the second person to ever receive a bachelor's degree in sculpture from that university."

From there she did a stint in the U.S. Coast Guard during WWII and returned home to marry an architect. Having worked with him on building designs, she later went on to design and build her own highly acclaimed structures, known for their innovative, artistic twists.

◀ *Serpent Form*, an abstract carved in western red cedar, has a place beside Lois's cabin. It stands 4½' high and is 1½' wide.

▲ Lois Hollingsworth outside one of her cabins.

Journal

In the year 2000, when I was working on a giant woodcarving on the Avenue of the Giants in northern California, a local person told me that my art was strikingly similar to Lois Hollingsworth's. A few months later, while I was still working on the same woodcarving, a maroon SUV screeched to a halt next to me; out of it popped an energetic older lady who gushed, "I've been by two times, and finally, on the third time, here you are!" Then she gave me a big hug. The same local who had spoken to me had passed on a photo of one of my chainsaw carvings to Lois. Apparently she had enjoyed it, judging by the enthusiastic welcome she gave me.

—Jessie

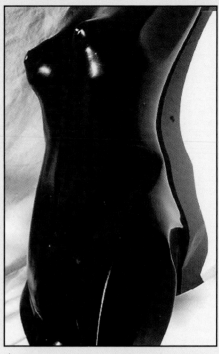

▲ *Face for a Friend* was carved in western red cedar. Here you can see the influence of the Haida natives of Queen Charlotte's Island in British Columbia. The artist spent some time with them refining her carving techniques. "They are the best woodcarvers in the world," she claims. Photo by Luke Finkelstein.

▲ *Torso*, carved in western red cedar, stands 3½' high by 2' wide. Lois says, "I carved the form in wood and then took it to an auto body shop to have them spray it with that black, shiny finish." Photo by Luke Finkelstein.

▼ Forms emerging from the rough in Lois' outdoor carving area by the stream.

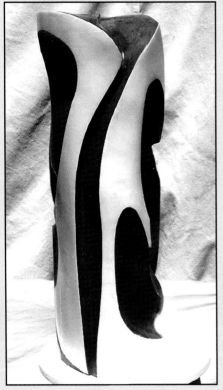 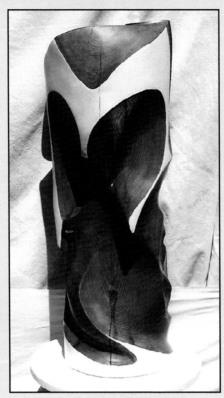 

▲ This sequence shows three views of one of the woodcarvings the artist describes as her "feelies." This tactile western red cedar piece stands 3' high by 1½' wide. Photos by Luke Finkelstein.

"I carved one into the rocky cliffs of Del Mar, and I built another house in Berkeley and one in Mendocino before I came out here and built the cabin I've been living in now for 33 years."

At home with nature

Lois Hollingsworth's cabin is located in an isolated area of rolling hills and oak trees high above the redwood giants of Northern California and is accessible only by a primitive one-lane dirt road. There she lives alone surrounded by the woods she loves and abundant wildlife.

"I used to have a pet bear and all kinds of animals that would come right up to the cabin. I think it's great living way out here this way. But I have two little dogs now that kind of keep the wildlife away from the door."

Relying on solar panels, a generator, and kerosene lamps, Lois still cuts up and burns wood as her only source of heat. In fact, it was cutting up firewood that actually gave her the idea of doing a chainsaw carving back around 1960, when the art form was almost unheard of.

"I first used the chainsaw as a tool to cut up firewood and build houses. Then one day I just started carving out an animal form with the chainsaw, and then more animal forms, and then abstracts. I love the effect the chainsaw has on the wood."

"You know, I used to be alone out there, but now there are quite a lot of people that do chainsaw carving. They sell it all up and down the highway. Mostly they make bears. I've never made a bear. I should probably try one," she laughs.

Today she calls herself a stylized abstract artist who creates sculptures just for fun. Over the years, her family and friends have become inundated with her unusual artwork. "So I recently started selling some of my pieces, but I really just do this for the love of it."

Lois Hollingsworth's carvings range in size from a three-inch goddess to a six-foot abstract, with western red cedar being her wood of choice.

"I like cedar best of all. But I also like any number of harder woods to do small pieces. Because when you're doing something small, you need a wood that's quite hard. It

depends on what I'm making and what I have on hand. I live in the woods so I have my choice of a variety of woods."

However, she is pretty picky when it comes to what piece of wood she chooses. It has to have some kind of a form or grain that interests her, and she doesn't like defects. "I'd rather not have any knots in my wood unless they add meaning to the piece."

Almost all of the pieces she does can be felt as much as looked at. This artist wants people to engage in her woodcarvings by having hands-on experiences. One of the best compliments she says she received was at a recent show, when a blind woman came in and fell in love with her work. "Even though she couldn't see it, she could feel it."

"My pieces are primarily tactile pieces—things to touch and feel and rub. People like to do that. I make human and animal shapes or some pieces that are just for feeling that I call my 'feelies,'" the artist explains.

She has also carved many bird forms—"guardian birds," she calls them. Usually she has a person in mind when she makes these guardian forms.

"I get my ideas from the wood. The wood dictates what happens to it. I work in a trance, and the wood dictates what I make. When I put my hands on it, that's when I get the idea. But it's up to the viewer to interpret the pieces. I wouldn't expect them to necessarily see what I see."

Most of her pieces are finished smoothly, but some are left rough. She finishes them in a variety of ways. Some of them have accents of color to make that surface stand out more than the others. She works many down really smooth with sandpaper, spending hours on a piece, and will even use her fingernails for finishing.

"Some have a very high finish so that they just glow, and others are left in the raw wood. Every piece is different just like every piece of wood is different."

Hefting a variety of chainsaws from large to small, Lois says she plans to continue carving for just as long as she can.

"I'll just keep going on and on, making things from what is here to make them out of. That's my life. It just goes on in three dimensions. You could say it in one sentence probably—Lois lived a three-dement-ional life."

Her advice to people is, "Get out there and do it!"

▲ Another beautiful form by Lois is her *Circles*, carved in western red cedar.

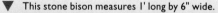
▼ This stone bison measures 1' long by 6" wide.

◀ *Bird Form* is an abstract carved in western red cedar. It stands 4½' high and is 2' wide.

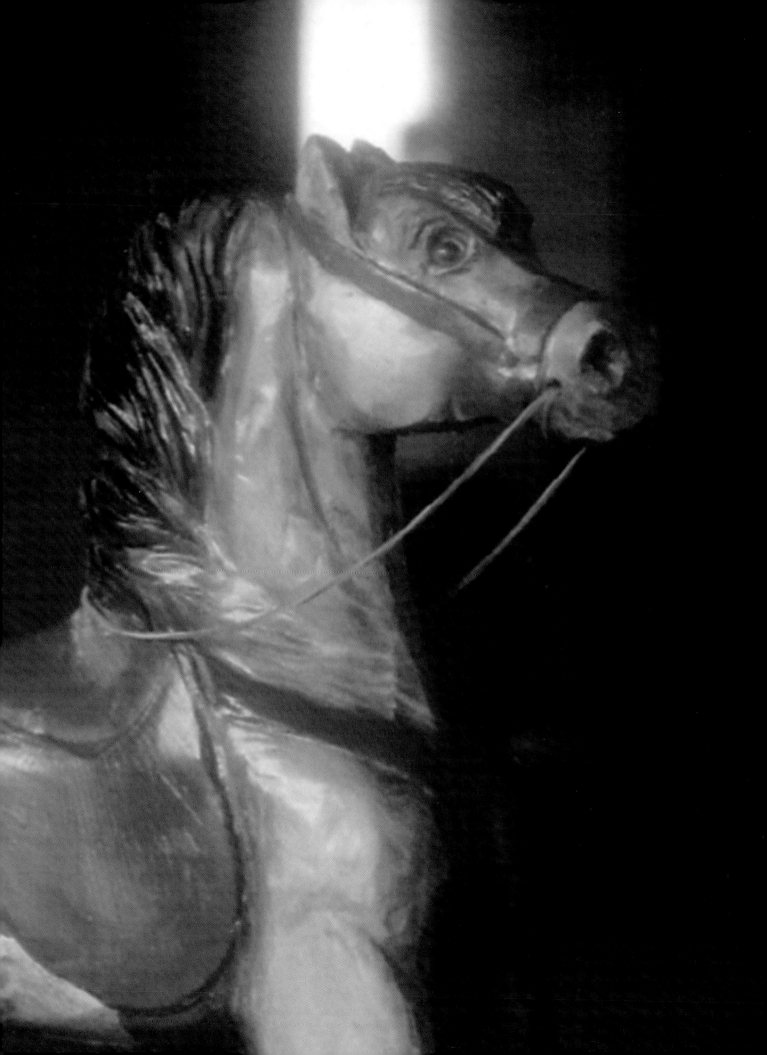

Susan Miller

MIST, OREGON

Looking at one of Susan Miller's carousel horses, you can almost hear the music and feel the excitement of your very first merry-go-round ride. Replete with detail and lavish hand painting, they are but a few of the hundreds of lively images that romp through this artist's mind and become immortalized in wood.

A pioneer in what was once perceived as a man's world, Susan's long love affair with wood has produced a wide array of intriguing projects. Through her early involvement with the Cascade Chainsaw Sculptors Guild, of which she was president from 2000 to 2004, and as editor of *The Cutting Edge*, she helped promote the art and lift it from its infancy to a recognized art form. In doing so, she etched her own name in the history books of chainsaw carving.

"Now that we have tools which make more intricate work possible, the community of carvers has grown," says Susan. "Contests and events have become an important avenue for exposing the art form to the public, and, in addition to the print medium, we now have the Internet to keep us all in touch. While being involved with all these changes is exciting, I am at heart a carver and would rather spend my time carving. What could be better than creating something that heretofore existed only in your mind—and making a living too?"

Many of Susan's carvings do not require a highly polished finish; others she lavishes with paints. Those are her favorites. "I love paint. I have fun with it. It seems like such a whimsical thing, and a lot of my carvings tend to be whimsical. If I hadn't become a carver, I probably would have been a graffiti artist because I am really good with spray paint," she laughs.

▲ Susan Miller sitting on one of her earlier rocking horses, carved in 1987. Photo by Pat McVay.

Journal

I get the sense that Susan is not really concerned with carving competitions. I think she would be perfectly happy whiling away the time in her beloved woods, chainsaw carving. Fortunately for us other carvers, she seizes events as opportunities to share her knowledge, techniques, and stories.

She told me that she enjoys hiking to far-away places in the mountains and making something large and attention grabbing from rocks or logs—something that stops a hiker in his tracks. She also likes to create small and half-hidden works of art from moss, bark, sticks, and seeds—something to make an observant person say, "Oh wow, who made this?" They may never know.

—Jessie

◄ *Rocking Horse* in western red cedar. Photo by Susan Miller.

▲ This is Susan's first carousel horse, created in 1995. Carved from basswood, the 4' figure is laminated to give the wood more strength. Prices for these run as high as $7,000. "This piece took me a long time. I wanted to do it because I love horses. Every time I got stuck and wasn't sure about something, I just went out and looked at my horses." Photo by Susan Miller.

◄ Susan working on her first carousel horse in 1995. Photo courtesy Susan Miller.

Against the odds

As a child, Susan displayed some obvious artistic talent through clay sculpting, sketching, and painting. But she was never encouraged to pursue art seriously.

"I grew up in a time when women were taught that they should be teachers or nurses, or have something like that to 'fall back' on. But I had worked at a stable helping to train harness racing horses, and what I really wanted to do was study veterinary medicine. However, the college I applied to told me that they did not take girls into the program, and I just accepted that."

In 1965, Susan immersed herself in teaching multiple-handicapped children at a school for the blind in Salem, Oregon. During that time, her aunt had started a little gift store. She had heard about a man who carved really nice things with a chainsaw and thought she might like to sell his work in her shop.

"She was a little bit reluctant to see some strange guy with a chainsaw and asked me if I would go with her," Susan recalls. "So we went together to visit Mike McVay. I saw his fantastic carvings, and I just couldn't believe it. I thought it was just so neat! One look and I immediately knew that this was for me—even though I had never in my life even picked up a chainsaw, or any other power tool for that matter. I told this to Mike, and he offered to help me get started. After a couple of sessions, I got some tools and started carving on my own."

Susan's first works were mostly relief pieces, primarily wall hangings of horse heads and such, with some tiki and owl carvings tossed into the mix. She learned early on to pay attention to the grain of the wood and use it as part of the design to create some lovely effects. But the progress of her carving was interrupted by other more adventurous projects, like getting married and building a houseboat in Alaska with her husband. She did, however, find new opportunities to experiment with her chainsaw.

"I tried carving a door for the houseboat. It looked great from the outside, but the wood inside dried and shrunk, and I had to stuff the cracks with paper towels and toilet paper. I also made a cradle for my son. We hung it from the ceiling, until a storm hit and the cradle kept crashing into the wall nearly tossing the baby out. We tossed the cradle (but not the baby) into the water, amused by the fact that someday some-

▲ *Fisherman*, cut from western red cedar, stands 7' tall. He was inspired by the wind. "I had been out on the river with the wind blowing, and I wanted to capture that feeling in this carving." Photo by Susan Miller.

one might find it washed up on the beach and wonder what story lay behind the cradle. A short time later, the house changed hands in a poker game and was towed upriver. The backside of the door no doubt surprised the new owner!"

After her marriage ended a few years later, Miller was left to raise two young children alone. She moved to Portland for a time; then someone told her how great southern Oregon was, so the young mother packed up her babies and headed for the hills.

▲ Hump's Restaurant in Clatskanie, Oregon, commissioned Susan to carve 17 panels in western red cedar for the outside of their restaurant in the late 1990s. Each detailed panel depicts life on the Columbia River in that area, both past and present. The project took two years to complete.

They were right, she discovered. It was a great place to live except for the fact that so many other people thought so too—housing was really scarce. She took on all kinds of odd jobs to make a living, such as carving and cleaning houses, anything and everything. But there just were not enough opportunities. Then, some friends offered to let her settle on their land way out in the country, and she jumped at the chance. Fascinated with the idea of a geodesic dome home, the energetic young mother decided to build one—herself.

"I had a taste of construction helping my husband build the houseboat, so I had a little bit of confidence. It was a simple structure made mostly of triangles. I used logs but I didn't have any power out there, so I could only used my chainsaw. I got pretty skillful with that little McCulloch Mini Max," she laughs.

"That's really when I began carving in earnest. I made everything we needed, sold what I carved, and grew a nice little garden. When I wasn't working, I enjoyed long walks in the wilderness teaching my children about nature. I traded some carvings for a car—an old rambler that had been in a

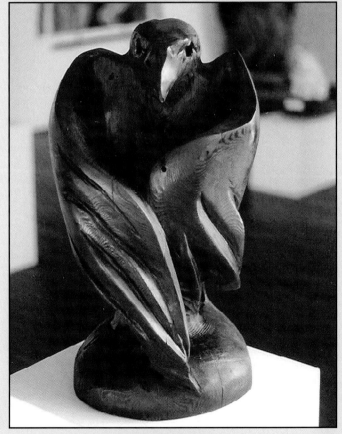

▲ *The Watcher* is a stylized bird that actually started out as a bear. "I cut the first hunk off and saw that bird in my mind." Photo by Susan Miller.

▲ Closeups of three of the panels for Hump's Restaurant. "This was my most ambitious project to date. I had to research and read a lot, study historical photographs, and talk to the local people who knew the history or the area in order to do that project." Photos by Susan Miller and Jessie Groeschen.

▲ Susan was commissioned to carve a bear leaning against a sign that read, "Do not feed the bears." Photo courtesy Susan Miller.

◄ *Guardian Bug* is part of Susan's personal collection. This western red cedar carving is an imposing 7' in height. It guards the gate to the artist's home. Photo by Susan Miller.

wreck. One door had to be tied shut with baling wire, and it wobbled down the road kind of crookedly, but it held a lot of carvings and just kept going and going for many miles."

When the kids got a little older, Susan moved to Eugene, Oregon, and attended the University of Oregon, majoring in art education. Later, she got her degree in elementary education and went on to earn a Master's degree in painting. All the while, her skills as a carver increased. She carved signs, did a lot of bears, fish, bookcases, cradles, rocking horses, simple furniture, and the standard whatever-would-sell kinds of things.

A carousel of creativity

With her children nearly grown, Susan began competing in chainsaw competitions, and her work took on dramatic new dimensions. The advent of her extravagant carousel horses marked a new direction for the artist. She unleashed her imagination and let her saw soar to new heights.

"I had been making rocking horses, and it just kind of evolved into the carousel horses. These are strictly commission pieces because they take so long and are such a tremendous amount of work, but I really enjoy it. They're about four feet high. I use basswood and do them like the traditional ones where they are hollow inside so they won't split as much. Then, I have to do a lot of laminating to make the legs strong enough. It's a tremendous amount of carving and sanding and painting. The last one I did had layers of translucent and pearl paints, and the flowers just kind of glowed."

Susan says it takes her longer to finish a piece than most of today's speed carvers. Her carousel horses are an example of that. "I'm not as productive as a lot of carvers are. I tend to get lost in detail. I tend to change things. I'm concerned with form. If I don't like how a piece is developing, I'll set it off to the side to work on other things. Then, all of a sudden, it will come to me what I need to do to change the piece I set aside."

Where does she get her inspiration? "I read a lot, and I dream a lot. I'll lie awake in bed early in the morning, and that's when I get most of my ideas. Still, a lot of times when I'm working on something, I won't have a clear idea in my head of what it's going to be. Then, all of a sudden, I just cut into that piece of wood and know what it needs to be. It's almost like a dialogue of what was inside of me and what was happening with the wood. It's between some subconscious part of me and the physical realities, and I love for that to happen."

"Other times, a client won't quite know what they want, and their uncertainty is my spark. Oh, that is fun, when this person I've just met provides some vague idea, and perhaps some money, and a place where the carving will go. It is quite an intimate thing to give form and reality to a person's dreams. And when you get it right, nothing feels better."

This artist also draws inspiration from her return trips to the Alaskan wilderness. Each summer, she travels there to

▲ Another one of Susan's rocking horses, carved in the early 1990s. She made a variety of other rocking animals at that time: pigs, chickens, bears, goats, and bunnies to name a few. These were carved in Douglas fir and basswood. Photo by Susan Miller.

renew her artistic reservoirs. Sometimes these trips bring an unexpected dose of reality.

"I was carving a life-size bear holding a sign that read 'Do not feed the bears' for a lodge that flew tourists in to eat fresh salmon. As soon as the salmon is cooked, the bears come swarming around looking for scraps, and the people inevitably throw them some. It was a problem because the bears were losing their fear of man. I was carving on the thing and had put my saw down to take a look at it when all of a sudden this bear comes around the corner and just stares at me. I've lived in Alaska enough that I'm really terrified of bears. So I grabbed the saw and yanked it to a start, and he ran back into the woods."

Today Susan Miller lives and works just outside the tiny town of Mist, Oregon, nestled in the highest elevation of Oregon's Coast Range, between Portland and Astoria. From the hill above her studio, she can see Saddle Mountain at the coast and watched Mount St. Helens erupt in Washington. At home with nature, Susan works a small farm with horses and enjoys an active life, hiking, horseback riding, and doing the thing she loves most: chainsaw carving.

Don Colp

OAKRIDGE, OREGON

A watchful pelican, playful bears, and soaring eagles come to life in the menagerie that has traveled with Don Colp around the country. During the peak of his traveling days, Don says that they logged 100,000 miles in 1974. "We do a wide range of carvings, but much of it is wildlife and early American stuff."

Don began woodcarving at a very early age, using a pocketknife while on his parents' farm. Out of necessity, he rapidly learned how to clear land with a chainsaw. He also owned and operated his own sawmill. In 1972, Don sold his sawmill and began chainsaw carving full-time.

"Chainsaw carving for me was a spin-off from the mill. I'd get up an hour early every day for work and would carve. I had about a half-dozen carvings that I did, I had them down to a science, and I learned to do them fast."

Speed, Don says, makes a big difference in the skill of the carver. "Carving at high speeds with the chainsaw is just like race car driving. You have to learn how to handle the tool at high speeds, and it makes you better at your day-to-day carving."

The Johnny Appleseed of chainsaw carving

In the mid-1970s through the late 1980s, Don would travel across the U.S. demonstrating his chainsaw sculpting skills at saw dealerships, fairs, and other openings. "They called me 'The Old Pioneer,'" Don laughs.

For his traveling rig, he converted an old school bus, cutting the top off the back portion so he could accommodate his larger carvings. He would eventually sell the bus to Conrad Sandoval, a young, budding chainsaw carver.

▲ Don working on one of his favorite subjects—horses—in 2003.

Journal

For years I heard Don's name in the chainsaw carving circle. One year in the mid-90s, he was a judge at West Coast, The Big One! (the annual chainsaw carving contest held in Westport, Washington). Everyone was really excited to have such an esteemed chainsaw carver as a judge. When I finally met him, I was apprehensive; usually I carve abstract sculptures, and Don is a cowboy-and-Indian kind of guy. What would he see in my unusual collection of broken seashells and suns chasing moons? My fears were unfounded; Don has a good energy about him, like a grandfather who cares for his chainsaw-carving grandkids.

—Jessie

◀ Don displays his fourth-place finish in the Pro Division at the Oregon Divisional Chainsaw Sculpting Championships in 2003.

Don Colp

▲ Don's son Mark poses with his third-place entry at Reedsport. Each of Don's three sons has been actively involved in chainsaw carving.

Like Johnny Appleseed, Don Colp planted the idea of chainsaw art in minds across America, inspiring and captivating his audiences with this new art form. A. J. Lutter, a full-time chainsaw sculptor, remembers seeing Don at the Minnesota State Fairgrounds in the early 1970s. "I stood with my mouth hanging open, like everyone else there," A. J. remembers.

It was during his demonstrating years in the 1970s that Don developed a chainsaw bar just for carving. He was demonstrating for Frontier saws, who came out with a hard-nose

chain bar. "I remember thinking, 'Now, if we can just get this bar tip a little narrower, we have something,'" Don says. He passed on his thoughts to Windsor Bar, who produced a bar designed to his specifications and idea. Thus, the quarter-size tip carving bar was born. But, in order to make his design a reality, he had to buy them in lots of 100 from Windsor Bar. And he did. Because it would take him years to go through 100 bars, Don starting selling them at his carving shows.

The bars did not sell quickly at first. Don's wife, Barbara, who placed the orders for the bars, remembers, "At first the bars didn't sell because they looked like they wouldn't hold up." Gradually, sales increased, and carvers would come from all over, buying half a dozen bars at a time.

Though the 72-year-old carver travels less than he used to, he still remains active in the chainsaw carving community. And he has made it a family affair: all three of his sons were carving before they got out of school. "I don't think any of them worked as anything other than chainsaw carvers. As soon as they got out of school, they worked for me in my shop," Don notes.

Mark, the oldest, who is well known on the circuit of chainsaw carving competition, has owned his own shop for 23 years. Brian is a partner with Don at their shop in Oakridge, Oregon. Matthew Colp, also a well-known chainsaw carver, passed away at the tender age of 20.

Don was also a well-respected judge on the West Coast chainsaw carving competition circuit until 2003, when he decided to enter his first contest—the Oregon Divisional Chainsaw Sculpting Championships. The contest, held annu-

ally on Father's Day in Reedsport, Oregon, featured Mark Colp that year as the returning champion. Father and son placed fourth and third respectively, a special treat for the two on Father's Day.

In 1992, Don moved to Oakridge, Oregon, with Barbara, and he shows no signs of slowing down. The family now has two small sawmills in addition to their shop and museum that houses vintage chainsaws, memorabilia, and carvings. Don still carves a number of different carvings—a great deal more than the half-dozen that he started carving in the 1960s and 1970s. "People come in and basically tell you what you want to make." Luckily, Don's favorites and what his customers want often coincide. He enjoys the early-American-themed sculptures—cowboys, Native Americans, and horses—and wildlife sculptures, especially salmon and whales.

Will he ever retire? "No, never," his wife attests. "He's just a goer, and I try to keep up with him." Truly the Johnny Appleseed of chainsaw carving, "Don is always willing to do what he can to promote chainsaw sculpting and help the carvers in the business," Barbara says.

▲ A 4' high by 3' wide redwood chainsaw carving by Matthew Colp, carved when he was 20. Behind the carving is the Grandfather Tree.

GUARDIAN SPIRIT

Judy McVay

DEMING, WASHINGTON

Every bit as vibrant and colorful as her trademark signs and murals, Judy McVay admittedly prefers adding color to her carvings, a trait that makes her work unique. "I like to paint, and it has kind of become my style. It makes my carvings stand out."

Interested in art from a very early age, Judy says that she was the artist of the McVay family. "I was always drawing and painting," she says. However, all of her siblings—chainsaw carvers Mike, Pat, and Eileen—certainly possess artistic and creative abilities, and each of them influenced the others. "They are all very talented," she notes.

Though she was always creating artwork, it wasn't until 1971 that Judy started carving with a chainsaw. After watching her older brother Mike carve during the 1960s, Judy took a lesson for the first time in the 1970s. "There were about three chainsaw carvers about the time that Mike was carving. Then, he taught us, and we helped out by burning and brushing the carvings." Soon, she started her own business, carving a wide variety of subjects including totem poles, flat pieces, wildlife, and ships. At this point, however, her pieces did not typically include a lot of painting.

In 1974, Judy moved to Whidbey Island and started a shop with her brothers, Mike and Pat, and sister, Eileen. "We carved a lot of furniture and were doing ten sets of bunk beds a week." The shop burned down in August of 1979. "After the shop burned down, everybody went their separate ways.

Journal

It was Thanksgiving in the early 90s when I was invited to Judy McVay's house. The fun began when the Pictionary game started. Two of her kids, Boaz and Lynn, were on the same team. Lynn drew a dot on the paper, and Boaz yelled out "universe" (which was the correct answer). They were really in tune with each other. But then, that is the type of connection that Judy's family has.

There is a very serious side to Judy: her carving side. She has been creating chainsaw art full-time since the early 1970s. It's fun to listen to her talk about her murals, which she puts her soul and heart into, and you can't help but be captivated. Her latest murals, combining Celtic weaves and Northwest native designs, are my favorites. She has blended her Irish heritage and the love of her modern home with striking results. They're like elements in a hand-sewn quilt—but Judy uses a chainsaw in place of a needle and thread.

—Jessie

▲ Judy's piece for the Northern California Championships held in Crescent City, California, in 2000, won third place. Judy says that she didn't come prepared to carve the bench made of redwood. "I didn't bring any tools with me because I hadn't planned on carving. But, when I got there, everyone wanted me to carve." Photo by Pat McVay.

◄ *Guardian Spirit*, Judy's contest piece for the Little Joe's Reno Contest in 2002, won sixth place. The piece measures 8' high by 7' wide and is made of ancient growth redwood. Photo by Pat McVay.

▲ Judy carved this queen-size bed, made of western red cedar, in the 1990s for the granddaughter of a fellow chainsaw carver, Paul Luvera. "He once told me that he was the only chainsaw carver with a carving on display on a naval ship. I said, 'I have to differ with you on that. I carved six totem poles for the USS Whidbey Island,'" Judy recalls. Photo by Judy McVay.

◄ *Springer Goes Home*, 5' high by 8' wide. This mural of Springer, the orca whale who was found in Puget Sound and released in Iceland, won Judy second place in the 2002 West Coast, The Big One! Photo by Pat McVay.

The only thing good that came from that was we pursued our art in our own way," Judy says.

For Judy, this meant going on to find her specialty—painted signs and murals, especially those that feature wildlife. "I didn't struggle to find my style; it just clicked. I love to do wildlife—that's what I do best. I've had people tell me that they can always recognize my work. Others have tried to carve what I do, but it doesn't quite work," she says.

"I prefer doing murals and signs, but I used to do a lot of standing things," Judy says. Of particular note are her totem poles. She placed fourth in the 1981 World Championships.

Carved in 1983 for the Red Rooster Tavern in Humptulips, Washington, *Olympic Peninsula Animals* is 16' long. Photo by Judy McVay.

Another of Judy's murals, *Whales, Dolphin, Elk*, measures 16' by 5'. The mural was carved in 1987 with only a chainsaw; then it was burned, brushed, and painted. The piece is displayed at the Ocean Crest Motel in Moclips, Washington. Photo courtesy Judy McVay.

North American Animals, which includes 70 animals, is 20' long and 8' high and was carved entirely with the chainsaw. This mural is the largest one in Judy's career. "I had to bend over and walk on the boards to cut it," Judy says. The wood is western red cedar. The piece is displayed at the Ocean Crest Motel in Moclips, Washington. Photo courtesy Judy McVay.

This page and opposite page: A selection of Judy's signs. Each shows her trademark style, especially in color and in portrayal of wildlife. Photos courtesy Judy McVay.

"You had to carve a 20-foot totem pole in six hours. After a few hours, you were just going on adrenaline, and once the contest was over, you'd just collapse." She also created six, five-foot-high totem poles for the USS Whidbey Island in 1986, making her one of the only carvers with her work displayed on a naval ship. She also made 14 signs, each with a different Northwestern animal on it, for the Whidbey Island Naval Air Station in 1996.

Wood as a canvas

To create her signs and murals, the largest of which is 20 feet long and 8 feet high, Judy uses an Alaska mill and a guide device, which is set up on a chainsaw with a long bar. This set-up enables the operator to cut straight boards. Then, she clamps the boards together and is ready to draw her designs, using a chainsaw to deeply illustrate the images. She finishes up with painting and burning techniques.

"I guess I'm really lucky that the painting comes out really well. You have to be careful with paints because you can completely screw up the painting. Most people tend to overpaint, and the carving ends up looking like plastic."

To give her carvings a natural look, Judy applies several coats of paint and wipes each one off. With this technique, she ensures that the wood still shows through the color.

More than just a masterful use of color, Judy's pieces also have a great sense of composition. "It's like painting a big picture. It has to have continuity and carry the eye around from one element to the next."

As a finish, paint also offers protection from the elements, something that is particularly important for signs and murals. Judy recalls one job in particular—a six-foot-high cedar sign—that the owner didn't want her to paint. "They didn't want to paint it, and when it's exposed to sun, rain, and weather, cedar tends to look like driftwood. You should be able to see a sign from two blocks away. Paint makes wood weather well."

Because of her skill at making signs, Judy was featured in *Sign Builders* magazine in 1995, who called her "The Queen of the chainsaw carved sign." She was also featured in *Woman's World* in 1983 for her art.

But the recognition she received at West Coast, The Big One! in 2002 is the experience that she talks about the most. For her *Springer Goes Home*, she took second place. Because West Coast, The Big One! is the largest chainsaw carving competition in the world, it's a great accomplishment to place in the top ten, let alone the top two. Judy is one of only two women to place in the top ten.

Also among her most-talked-about accomplishments and greatest pieces of art are her three children—Steve, Boaz, and Lynn Backus, all of whom are actively involved with chainsaw carving. This family of chainsaw carvers often travels to shows together and supports each other in the chainsaw carving community.

Though she has passed on her love of chainsaw carving to her children, Judy certainly isn't ready to retire. "I think I still have a few masterpieces in me," she says.

Brenda Hubbard

HOWARD, OHIO

▲ Brenda's bright, self-painted mode of travel, called the Sundance Express, served as a chainsaw carving rig that delivered her to chainsaw demonstrations.

Brenda Hubbard and her husband were going through the energy crisis in the early 1970s in Ohio when they decided to heat their home with firewood. Armed with chainsaws, they rummaged through the woods behind their home, sawing up limbs and trunks destined for the woodstove.

That's when Brenda noticed the beautiful color and grain of the cherry tree. In fact, she fell in love with the cherry wood pieces and decided they were far too precious to burn. Carefully collecting them and setting them aside at home, she challenged her husband to make some kind of carving out of the charming chunks, but for some reason the cherry wood did not speak to him as it did to her. Time went by, but she could not forget those pieces. The lure was too great.

No longer able to resist, Brenda Hubbard picked up her chainsaw and carved her first piece of cherry wood. Since

◄ *Johnny Appleseed* perpetuates the tall tale, standing 17' high at Mohican Campground in Mohican, Ohio. Photo by Rob Rouse.

Journal

I learned about Brenda Hubbard through an announcement of a benefit being held for her: she was in the advanced stage of cancer, and the chainsaw carvers wanted to help. I came across some pictures of her work; it was some of the best folksy chainsaw art I had ever seen. Though she was weak, I was able to speak with her on the phone, and she had time to tell me a bit about herself. I was moved that she also wanted to know about me—something I thought was very kind and gracious.

Brenda passed away during the making of this book. Although I never met her in person, I felt as though I lost a friend. She contributed to the chainsaw art scene in many ways by carving at fairs and saw dealership openings. She once said of the chainsaw carving family: "I feel proud and lucky to be part of such an independent, strong, and caring group of hard-working people who are crazy enough to risk their very lives; to endure the noise, the sawdust in their underwear, and the plain hard work involved in order to pursue their passion for this unique craft." Brenda—we were proud to count you among our numbers. We will miss you.

—Jessie

Water Lady is a life-size nautical chainsaw carving. Also shown is a realistic life-size *Ax Man* who looks as if he just lumbered out of the forest. Photo by Rob Rouse.

then, she dedicated much of her time to bringing out the life in the wood pieces.

Brenda Hubbard excelled at chainsaw carving to the point where she felt confident demonstrating her carving prowess at county fairs and arts and crafts festivals. At one time, Jonsered, a chainsaw manufacturer centered in Gothenburg, Sweden, sponsored her art.

"Whenever a saw would quit, they would just give me another one," she said.

In addition to performance carvings, Brenda also completed a number of commission pieces, peppered in and around her surrounding area in Ohio. One notable piece is a 17-foot-tall carving of Johnny Appleseed, located at the Mohican Campground in rural Ohio.

Prominent contemporary wood sculptor, Jerry Ward remembers talking with Brenda at great length about woodcarving, early in her career. "She was really excited about woodcarving and the direction her art was going in."

The mother of three said that chainsaw carving was a great escape from her quarreling kids; when they would start complaining about each other, she would just rev up the chainsaw louder. "They eventually would work it out between themselves," she laughed.

Many of her works are life-size, with some tending to be whimsical and caricature-like. Another striking feature is the soulful eyes of her pieces—right down to the animal carvings. Her favorite woods to work in were walnut, butternut, red oak, and, of course, cherry.

▲ *Gonna Bake an Apple Pie* stands alongside *Mr. Dog*. Photo by Rob Rouse.

◄ This is one of Brenda Hubbard's bench carvings. Photo by Rob Rouse.

> Part Two <

The Contemporary Artists

Through the pioneering efforts of the early artists, through books, and through shows and contests, chainsaw carving gained momentum, and the number of artists grew. The contemporary artists featured here have honed the skills and further developed the styles of the early artists. Whether their works are speed carvings or month-long projects, tiny birds to tall figures, each of these carvers' top-notch art composes the cutting edge of the art form.

J. Chester Armstrong

SISTERS, OREGON

Well respected as one of the great chainsaw carvers, J. Chester Armstrong creates powerful, compelling studies in energy. Their strength of form and primal beauty arouses and stirs the imagination. You can almost hear a stampede of pounding hoofs or powerful wings beating the air as he releases his spectacular sculptures from the natural grain of the raw log.

"I would call myself a classical wildlife sculptor," says J. Chester. "The fluid rhythm of lines, the symmetry of design, the energy and movement of a piece are all-important in my woodcarvings. I portray the tension of the animals and catch their emotions. The creative process is very exciting to me. I'm not just making a replica of the animal, some kind of artifact; I'm expressing something that has an inherent soul."

Flowing lines and rich patinas bring out the natural beauty of the dark woods he prefers most. They consist of woods native to the mountain wilderness of central Oregon where he resides, such as juniper, maple, and oak, with his favorite being black walnut.

"Black walnut has a lot of color, depth, and soul. It's a hard wood that's strong enough to hold the fine details of a carving, allowing me to do intricate things with it. That intricacy is important. It's the little accents that make a piece come alive."

J. Chester does not paint his pieces. Rather, he prefers to showcase the radiant colors of the natural wood. "My feeling is that wood itself is so beautiful you don't need to paint it. I want the grains to show through and the organics of that particular tree, the color that is unique to it. I will play with lights and darks sometimes but never a color. That would dramatically unbalance things."

Journal

I first encountered J. Chester Armstrong's work at the Moonraker Bookstore on Whidbey Island. I bought J. Chester's book, Chainsaw Sculptor, by Sharon Sherman, immediately and loved it. He spoke eloquently about the chainsaw, the wood, and what he was creating that I ended up buying three of his books to give away to chainsaw-sculptor friends.

When I called him up to ask if he would like to contribute to a book on the art of chainsaw carving, he instantly said yes. I drove the six hours from Seattle to his driveway in Sisters, Oregon, where I drove past black walnut logs strewn about. In the middle of the beautiful chaos was order: glorious black walnut horses, juniper eagles, and J. Chester Armstrong, speaking eloquently about nature and his art.

—Jessie

▲ Inside his studio, J. Chester proudly displays his recent piece, *Equine Thunder*.

◄ Carved in juniper, *Warrior Spirit* snatches up a catch of fish. The piece measures 8' high by 6' wide.

Predatory Instincts is a gripping, 2004 life-size sculpture that measures 5' high and 25" wide. For a more dramatic effect, the artist combined both black walnut and white cambium. "I wanted to convey the idea that the cougar is a force of nature, muscles tensed, stalking his prey." Photo courtesy J. Chester Armstrong.

At ¾ life-size, *Lord of the Range* rears up to its full height of 8' tall. "I carved that piece in 2003 in black walnut, which is one of my favorite woods." Photo courtesy J. Chester Armstrong.

J. Chester appreciates the balances in nature too, such as the relationship between man and trees. "We humans live in balance with the trees. We breathe out carbon dioxide and trees give off oxygen; it's a constant exchange. I just love that whole healthy cycle going on between trees and us. Wood is precious. Wood is dear. We have to have a respect and a reverence for trees that allow us to maintain the proper relationship," says the artist.

Because of his deep reverence for wood, J. Chester only uses dry, well-aged downed limbs and trees, never taking wood from standing live trees.

"I don't go to the forest and cut down the trees. Nor do I use trees that were cut down needlessly. The trees that I use had to come out for some other reason. So my thinking there is that I'm giving them a new life in a sculptural form. In nature those trees would have just deteriorated And gone back into the

earth. I'm taking the energy and essence of that wood out of the death cycle and putting it into a cycle that will last indefinitely longer—so in a sense I'm immortalizing that tree."

Early influences

J. Chester Armstrong grew up in the culturally rich environment of Berkeley, California, and graduated from the University of California with a degree in philosophy. He attributes his love of fine arts to two major factors.

"My mother was a world traveler with a great appreciation for art and a real love for wood. Wherever she went, she would always bring back things: masks from Africa, olive carvings from the Middle East, and Chinese and Balinese art, all in wood. Our living room was filled with these artifacts, and I always marveled at how they were made. I remember whittling as a child trying to duplicate some of them."

Wolfdreaming is a 1994 carving done in black walnut. It stands 3½' high by 20" wide by 20" round. This carving represents the duality of the male/female energy. The piece depicts a female shaman dreaming of her wolf-spirit protector. Photo courtesy J. Chester Armstrong.

Herons at the River's Edge is a 4' high by 14" wide sculpture in black walnut carved in 2002. "Attempting to capture the rhythm of the curved line was the inspiration for this piece. Herons always excite me with their prehistoric beauty and perfectly poised postures," says J. Chester. Photo courtesy J. Chester Armstrong.

The other experience that marked him so deeply was a trip to the Yucatan Peninsula. Traveling through the jungles, he stumbled upon some ancient Mayan temple ruins that were still encased in jungle.

"This was back in the early 1970s before they were touristized, and it was almost like I had discovered them because I wasn't actually looking for them. I wandered amongst these things and realized that the last remaining vestige of this whole culture was in their artifacts and carvings on the temple walls. And that just triggered something in me. I felt that if a person was going to lend their life's energy to something, it should have long-term, lasting value. Art was a way of doing that. It was a great eye-opening experience."

Continuing his travels, J. Chester loaded up his trusty old Volkswagen bus and worked his way up to Vermont where he earned a living clearing fields and repairing dilapidated barns.

During this time, the 22-year-old acquired his first chainsaw in trade for helping a farmer clear his back 40.

"It was an old Stihl, a relic of an ancient age, with solid cast iron parts that must have weighed a hundred pounds. It was a real beast. I had a tough learning curve with that old saw, but I used it for all these barn projects and odd jobs I ended up doing. It became my constant companion."

In college, J. Chester had hopped several freight trains going north, experiencing the rugged beauty of the West Coast from the back of a freight car, and loved what he saw. As soon as the young adventurer felt confident that he had gained enough real skills to make a decent living in the wilderness, he headed for the Pacific Northwest.

In 1973, he landed a job as a caretaker for the YMCA camp at Spirit Lake in Washington State at the foot of Mount St. Helens. There he was charged with rebuilding the

J. Chester Armstrong

camp, damaged during the Columbus Day Storm.

"Trees were down everywhere and some had crashed through the cabins, so there was a lot of work to be done. I had a chainsaw and a good knowledge of tools and motors and all those things that were needed to do the job."

It was not long before the ambitious young man advanced to the role of camp director. Wanting to introduce the kids to the Native American culture of that area, totem poles became the focus. He carved them and the kids painted them.

"I wanted them to have some lasting momento of their days at camp. There was that Mayan influence again and my belief that it's the artifacts that are lasting. That was the beginning of chainsaw carving for me."

With Mount St. Helens getting ready to blow, the camp was abandoned and J. Chester resumed the role of caretaker. For him it was a totally unique experience, never to be duplicated again, because this pristine lake and mountain setting turned into a fiery volcano, leaving the camp 200 feet under Spirit Lake.

"That last summer when I stayed behind to pack up the camp, I developed a real connection with the animals—bears, cougars, herons, and otters in the lake. I lived with them, and they became my companions, especially the otters. I would observe their playfulness and energy. Then one day, I had a revelation to carve the shape of the otter. It was then that I moved from the linear pattern of totem poles and entered a whole different world. By the time the snow fell, I had carved them all."

Preparing to leave, J. Chester loaded his many carvings into a boat, took them across the lake, and unloaded them onto the parking lot. In the time it took for him to walk back up the hill and get his car, a crowd of people, who were also packing up and leaving, had gathered around to ask him how much he wanted for this piece or that piece.

"It had never occurred to me to sell them. They were like my friends. But I realized that if I was really serious about sculpting, I had to learn to let them go. I sold all but one. From that point on, I never looked back."

▶ The stunning 2004 *Equine Thunder* is carved in black walnut and measures 5' long by 5' high. Photo courtesy J. Chester Armstrong.

◀ *Vision Quest* stands 8' high and 24" wide and was carved in lodge pole pine in 2002. In this depiction, the eagle represents the untamable wildness of the wilderness. Photo courtesy J. Chester Armstrong.

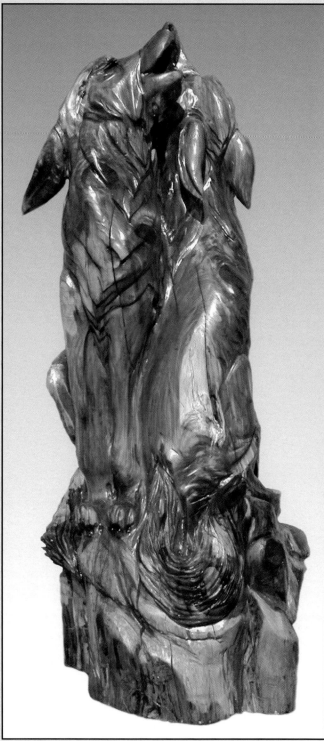

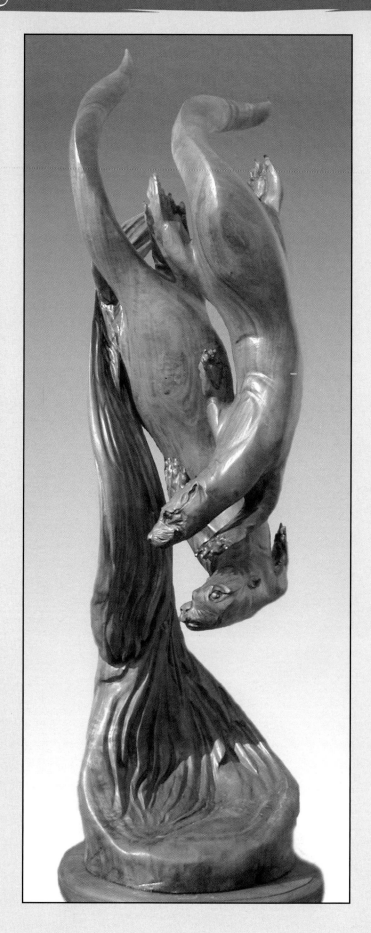

▲ Juniper was used for this 1999 piece called *Moon Song*. It measures 3' high by 16" wide. J. Chester says, "The night sounds of the high desert inspired this carving. I often hear the coyotes howling at the moon early in the morning and love their enthusiasm. This piece also represents the intertwining of the male and female spirit." Photo courtesy J. Chester Armstrong.

▶ This playful piece, called *Always Recess*, is 4' high by 20" wide. Created in 2004 in black walnut, it delightfully depicts river otters at play. Photo courtesy J. Chester Armstrong.

Folk art to fine art

Today J. Chester still lives and works in Sisters, Oregon, on the piece of property he bought before leaving the lake. Surrounded by seven snow-capped peaks and several wild rivers, the area is encompassed by wilderness.

"I just fell in love with this area and set up a little shop in downtown Sisters where there was a little traffic flow. I thought this would be a great place where one could practice one's art and make a decent living. I've been here ever since. It was a good choice," he chuckles.

Almost from the beginning, his carvings possessed elements that transformed them from folk art to fine art. Moving upward in the art circles, word of his work spread from the tiny mountain town to around the globe. J. Chester's work is featured in 15 distinguished art galleries throughout the Southwest.

"I think I was a little eccentric all along, and it just took life's experience to direct that towards art."

One of J. Chester's artistic approaches is to combine earth elements with the animal forms featured in his pieces. In his carving called *Sky Thunder*, for example, the artist combines the fire of the sky, which is the eagle, with air, water, and salmon, representing an endless loop.

"The important thing, I believe, is that the form of a piece should precede its subject. Form is the crucial factor that makes it art. The lines have to flow and interact. The rhythm of the line in a piece is really what I'm after. It's an important aspect because I'm not just carving a horse. I'm carving the rhythm of a line that is the back and neck and head of a horse. The multiple interactions of those rhythms become the sculpture. All those rhythms create an energy flow, a dynamic that comes out of the piece," J. Chester explains. "So there is more to this than just carving a piece. There is a sculptural quality to them that I think lifts them out of a folk art range into the fine art range."

Unlike other forms of fine art, however, chainsaw carving can lead to serious physical difficulties, such as hearing loss and loss of blood circulation in the fingers.

"Hearing loss is a total liability of the occupation. There is no way to avoid it. Even wearing the best earphones you can buy, you are still wearing out those ear follicles, and the result is that you become hard of hearing. The high-pitch sounds of tools and chainsaws have already wiped out a whole range of hearing for me. It's one of the sacrifices you make for this form of art," he explains.

"Not only that, but the constant vibration of the tools impairs the circulation of your fingers, giving you what is called 'vibration white finger,' which makes them painful and sensitive to the cold."

To combat muscle and back problems associated with chainsaw carving, J. Chester turns to yoga.

"Your back is the key element when chainsaw carving, and if you can keep those muscles limber and strong, then you'll really avoid a lot of injuries that would otherwise happen. If you don't keep up some kind of exercise program, you will, without a doubt, strain and pull muscles, especially as you get older. Athletes know what you've got to do to keep the body in shape, and, to some degree, I think chainsaw carvers have to pursue this same type of program."

Wildlife Artisans, J. Chester's studio, is generally open to the public. However, visitors are not likely to find any of this artist's work sitting around gathering dust. With half of them commission pieces and the others slated for galleries, his carvings fly out the door before the sawdust starts to settle.

J. Chester's pieces range in height from 12 inches to 20 feet and in price from $500 to $80,000 or more. Depending on the depth of the detail, they could take a day or even weeks to rough out. Then to actually refine them and finish them might take months.

"The real essence of every piece is the chainsaw. I go from big to little, using the big chainsaw to define my shape, and then the smaller saws to refine the shape, and so on down to routers. Then I use shaping tools to further define my sculptures."

But people do not seem to mind the long wait for J. Chester Armstrong's chainsaw carvings, and they do not mind paying top dollar either—just to get his signature. He suggests why.

"There is a gathering momentum for this kind of work out there in the world now. It's a new way of approaching art that's viable and sellable, and I think more and more people are recognizing that."

R. L. Blair

OCEANO, CALIFORNIA

You may not recognize the name, but chances are you have probably seen some of the extraordinary woodcarvings produced by R. L. Blair. In fact, it has been estimated that more than 30 million people view his work each year.

That's because R. L. Blair is the premier woodcarver for Disney, with his work scattered throughout all of the Disney-owned theme parks. From whimsical woodland creatures to trademarked animated movie characters to chipper chipmunks and big goofy bears, R. L. Blair's carvings captivate both young and old.

"I've been working with Disney since the mid-1980s, but you won't see my name anywhere. They want people to think that Tinker Bell made it or something," he laughs. "After all, it is the Magic Kingdom."

R. L. says that he enjoys this anonymity. It is enough for him just to know that in some small way his work has had an impact on the giant theme parks and has helped create the "Disney Magic."

"Some of the jobs are a pain in the neck, but most of them are a real kick," he says. "I do both parks here in California, both parks in Florida, one in Tokyo, one in France, and I just sent a whole bunch of stuff to Hong Kong. Now they're going to build another one in China, so I guess I'll have to get a good interpreter or try to learn Chinese!"

R. L. has been carving professionally for 35 years now on the West Coast, including a stint of carving with Duke Moore at the base of Mount Rainier in Washington. Shying away from the chainsaw circuit, he works in the privacy of his home studio, creating art for several commissioned accounts in addition to Disney. He describes himself as a

Journal

In 1994, I encountered R. L.'s shop as I was traveling back across the country in my VW Bus. Inside were some great busts of Native Americans and women and studies of faces that he had carved (as if he needed to keep practicing!). Although he's a slender man with a beard, this rugged guy has the sensitivity to carve beautiful women's faces. R. L. is a great storyteller and is full of witty one-liners; in some ways, that description applies to his carvings too.

—Jessie

▲ R. L. Blair in his studio in Oceano, California, with one of his carvings.

◄ Briar Fox and Briar Bear look for Briar Rabbit, who chuckles atop Briar Bear's club at Disneyland.

R. L. Blair's latest piece for Disneyland in California is a whopping 13-foot carving depicting the characters in the Disney hit movie, *Brother Bear*. R. L. Blair stands beside it along with his wife and business manager, Susan Blair. Photo courtesy R.L. Blair.

This life-size eagle is located at Splash Mountain at Disneyland in California and is an original R. L. design. Photo courtesy R.L. Blair.

woodcarver who uses chainsaws rather than a chainsaw carver who carves wood, and makes note of the distinction. And, although much of his work is whimsical, R. L. often carves other styles as well.

"This is a business, so I'll make whatever people want. I've carved a lot of realism, including human figures, animals, nauticals, cowboys, and Native Americans. I've carved tree houses with characters in them, and I've done some abstract art. But I guess my personal taste leans towards my warped humor, like making off-the-wall, goofy-looking people and caricatures. If I'm just out here burning up time, that's always what I end up making—goofy, off-the-wall stuff."

Finding his way

R. L. Blair grew up on farms and ranches in western Washington during the era of logging giant old growth trees. His lifestyle included rodeos and livestock with no television or electronic amusements. To pass the time in between chores and other responsibilities, he took to whittling.

"When I was a kid, I whittled and made all kinds of stuff with pocketknives for no reason other than my own entertainment. It was just something to do. All the kids today want instant electronic gratification, so nobody really takes the time to learn anything like that," he explains.

"I started off making slingshots and toy guns, but it wasn't viewed by myself or others as being something extraordinary because everybody did all kinds of things. I mean my grandma went out and built fences and a well house and a pantry. Everybody was real handy like that. In fact, when I finally got old enough to date girls, I thought there was something wrong with them because you couldn't talk them into doing any of that stuff!"

When R. L. was about twelve, he experienced a life-altering event. While at a craft show in Olympia, Washington, he saw the work of an artist/professor named Philip McCracken who did wood carvings.

"His carvings were selling like crazy. I knew even then that I could do what he was doing. And that was the first time it clicked with me that this stuff had a value. I never did meet that guy, but if I could find him, I'd call him up and thank him because he turned my head around and made me look at my art in a whole different way."

These photos are part of the William Shatner collection. The figure on the right is life-size; the *Indian Chief* stands 7' high and is 4' wide. Photos courtesy R.L. Blair.

R. L.'s grandmother recognized artistic talent when she saw it and took an interest in the boy's art early on. She dragged him around to juried art shows where he won many awards in some tough handcarving competitions and even sold some of his pieces. In high school, he enjoyed art and excelled in art classes, but he resisted the input of others.

"You get teachers trying to teach you that the only way to paint a barn is their way, and that's red. Well, what's wrong with a kid going out and painting it green?"

As he grew older, the lure of the logging industry grew stronger. At 16 years old, R. L. decided to try his hand at it and was introduced to the chainsaw for the very first time.

"I ended up a logger just because it's a common occupation out there. And it pays a lot more than a burger place or a gas station because of the risk involved. I used to spend summers in fire suppression camps fighting forest fires, clearing trails, cutting down trees, and all kinds of stuff like that. Not logging per se, but the same as."

After high school, he moved way up on the Olympic Peninsula and went to work at a couple of shake mills and some of the bigger logging companies.

"There wasn't much industry up there. Everybody either worked in the woods or they fished or something of that nature. Logging is real hard work, and you burned out quick, so I didn't do any of it for an expanded length of time. It was just a fast way to earn a lot of money."

All the while, R. L. kept up his whittling every spare moment he had, and it kept improving. It was not until the 1970s that he started using the chainsaw himself for woodcarving and married his wife Susan. That's when his career really took off.

"I used to travel around and live out of my hip pocket. I worked for half a dozen chainsaw companies, and I'd go to all the county fairs and do all that showboat stuff. But now I like this staying-out-of-sight thing. I am not an entertainer. I see myself as a woodcarver. Period. No carving in public or showmanship here."

▲ "They opened up a section of the park at California Disney Adventure where they tell stories. All of these carvings are based on the stories that tell of the mythological beliefs of different tribes. The plaques tell what the story is about. It was a fun, challenging group of carvings to do." Carved in redwood, they are all about 7' high (or more) by 3' wide.

Turning a hobby into a business

It did not take long before word of his talent reached the ears of someone at Disney, and one job quickly turned into hundreds, jump-starting his career. Since then, he has carefully selected other accounts to whom he supplies carvings on a regular basis. He also takes on commission projects like the recent one he did for William Shatner (of Star Trek fame), landscaping his ranch in California.

Today, R. L. still lives and creates in relative seclusion. He and his wife, Susan, work together as a team. She takes care of the business end of things while he creates the art. R. L. jokes, "She uses one side of her brain and I use the other, so together we're like one whole person."

R. L. is also a proud father; he has two daughters, Stacie and Brandi, and one son, Travis. "Fortunately all of them have pursued normal lives," he chuckles.

Looking around his home and studio, you would be hard-pressed to find his artworks. That's because more often than not, as soon as they are done, they head out the door to either the client or the account.

"I don't save stuff. I don't collect stuff. My enjoyment is having somebody else enjoy it. If they buy it and they're happy with it, then that's great."

And although his woodcarvings are enjoyed by millions, R. L. is still reluctant to call himself an artist.

"I'm always kind of jumpy about the term 'artist.' I'm not sure what that is, but I've always enjoyed anything creative. I always excelled in art classes because I personally enjoyed it. And, if you enjoy something, then you're going to have more enthusiasm for it than the average person," he concludes.

"I still really enjoy the old traditional handcarving, but unfortunately you don't get paid for your time investment. It was the introduction of chainsaws and all of the high-tech power equipment that we use in this day and age that makes it possible to make a living at it. The chainsaw is a very valuable tool in my array of woodcarving tools. I'm always very respectful of that equipment. I have pocketknife scars on my legs that are 50 years old from whittling when I was a kid, but nothing major since then. I've got a lot of serious equipment that's designed to cut something but preferably not me."

When not working on wood projects, R. L. enjoys other kinds of art as well, such as oil painting, pottery, lead glass, blown glass, and steel. "I really like the process of creating things. It's just so much fun to mess around with all that stuff, but wood is my bread and butter."

Throughout the years, R. L. has used all kinds of wood for his carvings, whatever was necessary to get the job done or to create a specific effect. His preference, however, and the wood he uses most frequently, is redwood. He has truckloads of it shipped down to him from northern California. He prefers this wood because of how well it holds up outdoors and because he likes its giant size.

Because much of his work is commissioned, R. L. often has to recreate a specific character in wood and to work off photographs of that character, person, or animal. He has become very proficient at that.

"If it's something I've never carved before, I study pictures and nature. Say, for example, it's a bird; I try to figure out the mechanisms of how that bird sees and eats and flies. I create a mental picture and memorize it. Then I go out and carve it."

R. L.'s pieces range in size from about one foot all the way up to 18 feet, with many falling in the 7-to-12-foot range. The bulk of his work is sculptures with some elaborately carved signs thrown in. Recently, he completed a 14-foot carving of the bear characters in the delightful Disney movie *Brother Bear*. The carving features one huge bear sitting on a stump with the smaller bear perched playfully on his head.

"People tend to relate size to value, so I stay away from anything really small. You can make a big piece of junk, and it'll sell. But if you have something with extremely fine craftsmanship that you can hold in your hand, people are thinking $29.95. It doesn't matter if it took you three times as long to make it. It doesn't make sense; it's just a psychological thing. People think bigger is better."

One look at his art and it quickly becomes obvious why R. L. Blair is so successful. But his philosophy about himself and his art might also be a key to that success.

"I believe that it's easier to go through life underrated than overstated. Good is great; perfect, impossible. Work hard with dedication and who knows, maybe you'll get somewhere in life."

▲ California Disney Adventure features carvings for the Rushin' River Outfitters.

Edith Croft

ST. JEAN PORT JOLI, QUEBEC, CANADA

The leap from stroking a paintbrush to hefting a chainsaw proved an easy one for Edith Croft, who loves the speed, power, efficiency, and violence of the chainsaw. After many years of sculpting wood almost exclusively with a chainsaw, she now combines her mold-making and welding skills with her chainsaw carving skills to create highly unusual sculptures.

"I try to carve an actual social reality, a universal feeling into the flesh of a tree with a chainsaw. Using this implacable tool, I wound the wood to sketch the shapes of contemporary human drama."

Applying bronzing techniques to her chainsaw forms, she captures the texture of the chainsaw and meshes it together with new elements to complete her stylistic wood sculptures. Her favorite subject is the human body.

"The human body in its most primitive form inspires my creative works. In attempting to embed human shapes into the fibers of a tree, my sculptural creations convey the human cycle in its entirety, the emotional states traveled in human life from birth to death. My sculptures try to tell the story of humanity through an aesthetic object, which serves as a reflection of humanity itself," says the artist.

Even as a child, Edith Croft loved art and always involved herself in it one way or another. She particularly enjoyed drawing and painting. In high school, she was in charge of theater sets and would design and paint backgrounds and sceneries.

Edith entered Laval University in Quebec at 18 years old as an art major. At first, her interests were limited to painting. Then, after discovering three-dimensional materials, she dropped painting and immersed herself in sculpting. A short time later, while taking a woodworking class, she fell in love with the beauty and versatility of wood and began carving wood sculptures.

▲ Edith Croft at a gallery exhibit of her work.
Photo by Jean Marie Villeneuve.

Journal

Edith came to Whidbey Island with Pat McVay in the early 90s. They had met at a stone sculptor's symposium, and he invited her to the island. When Pat introduced us, we immediately became friends. She is from Quebec, and, although at that time her English was limited and I spoke no French, we somehow communicated through art and woodcarving.

She stayed for about two weeks, traveling with us to the West Coast, The Big One! Then, it was time for her to head back to Quebec to get her Master of Arts. We stayed in touch for the next two years. Then, one of her letters announced that she was driving to the West Coast with her dog and a friend. When she arrived in 1996, I offered her a place to stay during the transition from the university world to the non-university world. During those three months, we lived on the beach of Whidbey, collecting driftwood and branches to transform into art. When I see Edith's work today and her addition of found objects, it reminds me of that time period.

—Jessie

◄ The Weeping Willow Woman was carved from a pine log. The long white skirt and arms (up to the elbows) are carved in wood and coated with an epoxy resin. The weeping willow branches that protrude from her back are made out of bronze and iron. The bust is done in bronze. This 2003 commission piece stands 10' high. Photo by Ivan Binet.

Edith Croft

Cry Me a River, carved from cedar, with paint and a steel armature. This 2003 piece stands 12' high. "All of these feathers were made with a chainsaw, and then I put them together with eyed screws." Photo by Ivan Binet.

Solo exhibition of *The Angels Fall* at The Red Gallery in Quebec, Canada.

In 1990, a suggestion from an onlooker changed the direction of her art. Edith had been hard at work for days trying to chisel out a large wooden sculpture. A friend who was intently watching this painfully slow process suggested that Edith might be better off using a chainsaw—a thought that had never occurred to her. So she bought her first chainsaw and began experimenting with this new and exciting approach to wood.

"I immediately loved the chainsaw for its speed and the texture it leaves on the surface of the wood. It became my favorite tool."

Trying to locate a good piece of wood to carve while at the university proved a difficult task for the burgeoning young artist. That is, until she came up with the brilliant idea of ordering a truckload of telephone poles.

"I learned that you can get them fairly cheap, so I ordered a whole truckload of telephone poles and had them delivered to the university."

Edith used nine of those telephone poles for a grouping called *The Savage Cathedral* in 1994. This creation was made up of nine human bodies about 10 feet high, all carved in yellow cedar and standing close to each other to form a human architecture. The surprise was in its shocking completion.

"I wanted to go further with this piece than to just use the tool. So I took them to the beach, planted them all out in the sand, poured gas all over them, and ignited them. As the human part of the sculpture was burning, this sculpture was entering into a silent eternity. The ensemble was then exhibited in several galleries smelling like burned wood. Each body was then sold separately even though they had become very fragile. I made a video of the burning sculpture. It was a good meditating moment and still is."

The Savage Cathedral is a 1994 ensemble of nine 10'-tall human figures carved in yellow cedar, doused with gasoline, and set on fire to add further artistic expression. Each figure was then sold individually. Photo courtesy Edith Croft.

After receiving her bachelor's degree from Laval University, Edith was awarded the Merit of Excellence, a substantial grant from the Canadian government to continue sculptural research for her provocative art. This grant enabled her to travel to the west coast of Canada to continue her research for her master's degree.

She spent the summer on the west coast of Canada. Her research later brought her to the U.S., where she participated in a popular woodcarving event known as West Coast, The Big One!, held in Westport, Washington, in 1994. There, she discovered a real diversity in chainsaw carving techniques, which she seamlessly adapted to her own work.

Later that same year, Edith traveled to the opposite side of the globe to Zwickau, Germany, to participate in a different kind of woodcarving event, an International Wood and Stone Sculpture Symposium.

In 1996, her sculptural research propelled her from Quebec to British Columbia, where she immersed herself in the study of the western Canadian native people, their cultures, and their carvings. She spent four years in the city of Vancouver.

"I am especially interested in the tradition of totem poles. My research focused on the symbolic meaning of the totem, namely the power expressed through its physical form, the respect it demands by its massive proportions, and the ancestral myths that permeate its very fibers. I wanted to grasp the aesthetics of this culture to feed my own sculptural creations," she explains.

"I sought not to simply reproduce traditional images inspired by Gitkan and Haida cultures, rather to achieve an understanding of the spirit and symbolism of totem traditions to bring forth other imagery, closer to contemporary reality. In this way, my creative effort would investigate totems in their deepest sense, producing a sculptural work bearing a new social mythology in a form that engages the emotions of the observer."

In 2000, Edith returned to her roots in Quebec, where she and her spouse purchased 106 acres of land out in the country. It is in this isolated location that they plan to build their permanent studio.

"The country isolation is good for the soul and for the creative process."

Today Edith continues her brazen style of sculpture. Her work has been included in a number of solo, duo, and group exhibits throughout Quebec. She works in the movie industry as a sculptor and a mold maker in Montreal and teaches sculpting at an art college in Québec City.

With the majority of her works carved in cedar, Edith's pieces are quite large and are not intended for outside display. However, *Weeping Willow Woman* was an exception. She was a commissioned piece specifically designed for the outdoors.

"I had to take special precautions to protect the wood from the UV rays. It required the application of 12 different coatings."

Edith is not entirely certain what direction her art will take in the future, but she says there is one thing we can be sure of—her love of wood will never diminish.

◄ *Although His Wings Have Turned to Stones* is a 2003 sculpture measuring 12' long and 10' wide. The materials are wood and slate. "The lower body of this person is made from branches that I collected on the seashore. They are whitewashed from the salt water, and I wove them all together. The upper wood body is a chainsaw carving. I put back a piece of bark on his arm for effect. The stone wings are made of slate arranged in wing shapes." Photo by Ivan Binet.

Glenn Greensides

SAYWARD, (VANCOUVER ISLAND) BRITISH COLUMBIA, CANADA

Glenn Greensides is often soft-spoken and understated, but only one word can describe his art: monumental. Many of his carvings measure at least 16 feet tall, and each carving is meticulously detailed and refined.

However, Glenn hasn't always been carving pieces on such a massive scale. Born in Toronto, Ontario, Glenn settled in British Columbia in 1982 and used the chainsaw for many years as a log home builder. After seeing a few chainsaw carvings here and there, he decided to give carving a try. "Before that experience, I never used a chisel or a knife, but I did draw a bit."

"Working as a log home builder from 1982 to 1987, I developed my skills with chainsaws and rotary tools. After seeing a few chainsaw sculptors, I was inspired to apply my acquired skills. The first attempts were small cartoon characters and wildlife themes," Glenn says.

In 1990, his friends encouraged him to go to the Prince George Forestry Exhibition and display some of his carvings. "During that show, I was approached by Husqvarna chainsaw reps, who invited me to demonstrate my art at the Pacific National Exhibition in Vancouver. I went on to do performance demonstration art at saw dealerships, openings of stores, and logger shows. In a sense, I started off as somewhat of a street corner artist," Glenn recalls.

Between shows, Glenn worked on small commissions, and he eventually started getting bigger commissions for resorts and businesses. But he found the unstable flow of work and money discouraging. His solution: to find his own market carving large-scale pieces. "I enjoy working on larger pieces, and I like the idea of not spending as much time looking for work."

Glenn also began moving away from the wildlife and cartoon carvings that he first carved. By his second year of carving, Glenn was beginning to experiment with human figures.

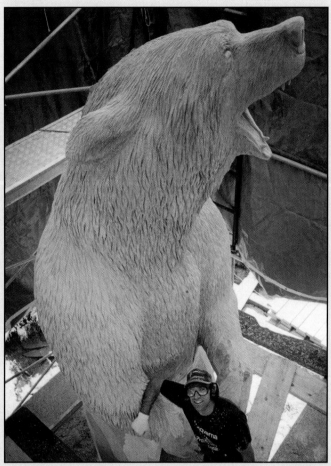

▲ Glenn and his 16' grizzly bear carved at the Pacific National Exhibition 1995. The carving later became part of the Tribute to the Forest collection on Grouse Mountain. Photo courtesy Glenn Greensides.

Journal

I first encountered Glenn's work at Grouse Mountain in the mid-90s. Glenn's art is really, really big. It showcases the size and stature of the giant Douglas fir trees that grow in BC. Right away, I knew that he was no ordinary chainsaw sculptor. Many years later, I was able to meet this woodcarver who has such genuine passion and drive for his art.

—Jessie

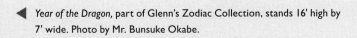

◀ *Year of the Dragon*, part of Glenn's Zodiac Collection, stands 16' high by 7' wide. Photo by Mr. Bunsuke Okabe.

These five sculptures are the last ones that Glenn created for the Tribute to the Forest Collection. This photo was taken in 2004.

Promotional photo for Finning, one of Glenn's sponsors for Tribute to the Forest. Carved Logger stands amongst salvaged dead standing trees provided for future sculptures. Photo by Stan Rhompf, 1994.

Glenn Greensides' towering woodcarvings set him apart from other carvers not only because of their sheer size, but also because of their numbers. This artist has an affinity for creating collections of large-scale pieces, and the pieces in each collection are bound together by a common theme. "It's about storytelling really. Most of my collections tell about forestry heritage and human-interest themes. Humbled by the enormous trees, I decided to promote the idea of making heritage-themed sculptures that depicted forestry-related messages to the public. This, in turn, opened the doors to sponsorship from coastal logging companies who supplied many of the logs needed for my projects."

"I found myself drawn to satisfying the needs of the public who view my art. Since the trees that I wanted people to experience were, by many, considered best left untouched, I searched for logs that fell under the following criteria: dead standing trees or salvaged logs from the pulp grade market with severe twist, therefore unsuitable for making lumber."

His Tribute to the Forest is located at the peak of Grouse Mountain in Vancouver, British Columbia. The 31 sculptures focus on the positive roles that humans play in our forest ecosystems. His depictions include anything from a woman planting a tree to a firefighter who helps to control forest fires—showing the variety of ways in which we interact with forest environments. The average height of each sculpture is 16 feet, and they range from five to nine feet in diameter. Twenty-one of the 31 wood sculptures depict human characters; the other ten depict wildlife. It took Glenn seven years to finish the collection.

Three 16' figures, depicting outdoor recreation, are part of Glenn's Tribute to the Forest Collection at Grouse Mountain in north Vancouver, British Columbia. The photo was taken in 1997. Photo courtesy Glenn Greensides.

▲ *Forest Renewal*. This 12' sculpture depicting a logger, tree planter and eagle was originally on display in the Forest Alliance Information Center in Vancouver. It now is located at the Mountain Retreat Hotel in Squamish, BC. Photo by by Naomi Stevens, 1993.

▲ The spruce bark beetle depicting another destructive force in nature.

◄ Three sports figures depicting sports that utilize wood products; a subtle reminder that we are closely connected to forests in many different ways. Photo by Glenn Greensides.

Glenn Greensides

In 1995, Glenn started his second major collection of work. Located at Japan's Listel Inashawiro Hotel, the collection requires the artist to visit Japan once a year for 12 consecutive years. The series is set to be completed by 2008. "Each year, I create one five-meter-tall sculpture from an exported British Columbia log, depicting the upcoming year's Japanese zodiac symbol. I feel honored to have such a meaningful project that reflects the Japanese culture and their appreciation of wood and art," Glenn says.

▲ *Year of the Horse* resides at the Listel Inawashiro Hotel in Inawashiro, Japan. Photo taken in 2002 by Mr. Tadahiko Ogawa.

◀ *Year of the Tiger* resides at the Listel Inawashiro Hotel in Inawashiro, Japan. Photo taken in 1998 by Mr. Kiyotaka Suzuki.

▲ Log book structures await relocation where they will then be landscaped with wild plants and tree species found in the coastal forests of British Columbia.

Storytelling on a grand scale

Glenn's latest project is Log Book Park, a heritage attraction in Squamish, British Columbia. The idea of Log Book Park developed out of a deep appreciation and concern for the rich forest heritage in British Columbia. The collection is part of a project that will develop into a forestry theme park in the Squamish District.

"I have created a collection of 14 giant, wooden books depicting the history of British Columbia's west coast forests. Each log has been first cut in half, and then stood on end to represent the cover of each opened book. Attached to each halved log are carved laminated panels, which depict the history of British Columbia's forest from the prehistoric era to the present day. Each book will be protected with a wooden roof, designed to symbolize the flowing canopy and branches of a tree."

Glenn's next project is in a somewhat different vein—he and his wife, Elizabeth, plan to build their own house and studio on their four acres of riverside property in Sayward, British Columbia. Though the house-building project will certainly take up some of his time, Glenn says that he will find time to work on his carving, "I plan to continue working on heritage themes focusing on human portrayals."

▲ Two carved wooden pages will be attached to each of the 14 log books once the site is prepared. The 28 pages took Glenn one and a half years to complete.

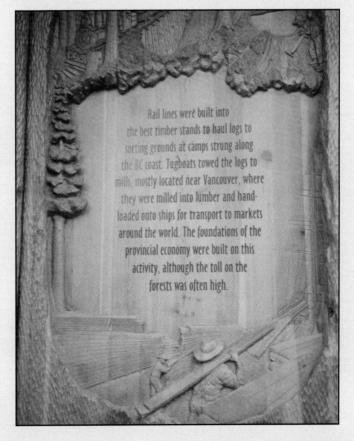

Rail lines were built into the best timber stands to haul logs to sorting grounds at camps strung along the BC coast. Tugboats towed the logs to mills, mostly located near Vancouver, where they were milled into lumber and hand-loaded onto ships for transport to markets around the world. The foundations of the provincial economy were built on this activity, although the toll on the forests was often high.

▶ One page from the log book collection in Squamish, B.C. The script for Glenn's log books was written by author Ken Drushka. Photo courtesy Glenn Greensides, 2003.

PAUL BUNYAN TALE
BEARS FILLED THE FOREST IN
PAUL'S DAY. PAUL MADE A PET
OUT OF ONE AND TRAINED IT TO
WALK ON ITS TWO FRONT PAWS
CARVED BY - A.J. LUSTER
DONATED BY-PAUL BUNYAN CENTER

A. J. Lutter

BRAINERD, MINNESOTA

If any chainsaw carver could make you smile, it would probably be A. J. Lutter. That's because A. J. starts out every piece with the express intention of evoking just that—a big smile. More whimsical than serious, and even a bit cartoonish at times, his lighthearted carvings burst with energy and flow with motion.

"There are two things I want my work to do—look like it's in motion and make people smile. That's what I've been shooting for all these years, besides selling the piece," laughs the 55-year-old carver. "There are a lot of pretty good carvers out there, but their work is often stiff and lifeless, with no action to the piece. I like a lot of movement and flow. If the piece has motion to it, it tends to hold people's attention. Then, if you can make them smile, well, that's like 75 percent of the sale right there. So that's what I try to do."

Well known for his whimsical bears, the artist has created more than 10,000 of the delightful creatures over the span of his 25-year career, plus thousands of other carvings ranging in size from two inches to a whopping sixteen feet tall.

"Bears have become one of my favorite subjects because they are so much fun. You can humanize them so easily with just a smile or a goofy grimace. They're pretty popular too. I can carve them in a variety of postures and expressions, and they all eventually sell."

A. J. draws much of the inspiration for his art form from the works of Norman Rockwell, an artist he greatly admires.

"At first glance, Norman Rockwell's art seems so simple, but the more you study his paintings, the more details jump out. All those subtle little things add up to portray a powerful scene. That's what I like about his work," says A. J. "I also like the fact that he was a production painter in a sense, creating so many covers for the Saturday Evening Post. He combined what he loved with making a living, and that's really important when you have a family."

▲ Visiting bikers might be surprised to discover a resemblance to this *Harley Gothic* caricature. Cut from white pine and hand painted, the life-size couple stands 5' high by 4' wide. Photo by A.J. Lutter.

Journal

I met A.J. on the ferry to Whidbey Island in the early 90s. He struck me as a good guy who was willing to help any carver who needed advice. Because of A. J.'s dedication to his fellow carvers, he is well-respected in the chainsaw carving world. He is responsible for organizing Garyway, a chainsaw carving auction to help pay the medical bills of chainsaw carver Gary Patterson. Over 30 chainsaw carvers made the trek to Sullivan, Missouri, to help Gary out, while many other carvers from around the nation shipped carvings for the auction. Gary held on until the event was over and then passed away exactly 24 hours later.

—Jessie

◄ *A Paul Bunyan Tale.* "Bears filled the forest in Paul's day. Paul made a pet out of one and trained it to walk on its two front paws." This quote is from the sign on A. J.'s bear, located in downtown Brainerd. This impressive 16' carving is made from white pine.

Inside A. J.'s Come See What I Saw Gallery, visitors are greeted by chainsaw carvings of all shapes and sizes—from his renowned bears and cowboys to flying horses and gnomes.

Rebecca, The Water Carrier measures 3' high by 2' wide. This carving typifies the action and movement for which A. J. is famous. You can almost see her skirt swishing and the water sloshing.

This foot-stomping Country Western Band ensemble is carved from white pine.

On the other hand, A. J. feels too many details can bog down a chainsaw carver. According to him, balance is the key to success.

"My theory has always been 'do the best you can, but keep the overall picture in focus.' Don't get lost in details. Some people want it to be absolutely perfect with not a hair out of place or anything like that, and, to me, that's not the objective. My objective is to make a living at this, and that means doing a nice job efficiently enough that I will be able to make money and build a good name and reputation at the same time."

The hungry years

For A. J. Lutter, the road to fame and fortune proved a dark and dreary journey. Like many Vietnam veterans, A. J. returned from the war confused and disgruntled with society. Seeking to get away from it all, he plopped down his savings on 80 acres of land in rural Minnesota and headed for the woods.

"I was trying to get away from the rat race, not realizing that the rat race is the only race and that's where the money is. I spent years bouncing around from job to job. Eventually, I became unemployed, and I thought, 'What am I going to do? I'm in the poorest county in the state, and there are no jobs to be had.' Things got tough, and then they got tougher."

One day, while walking through an area mall with his wife and two small girls, he chanced upon the Viking Woodcarving Show. It reminded him of how much he had enjoyed whittling in high school. He lingered over the displays and even sat in on a demonstration. When he got home, he dug out an old hacksaw blade, wrapped tape around it to fashion a handle, and began whittling.

"I discovered that whittling helped me keep my mind off my problems. I'd whittle whenever I got especially stressed out because being able to concentrate on something was a great relief to me. In fact, I enjoyed it so much I thought maybe I should try making a few bucks at this."

A. J. whittled like crazy, creating all kinds of little pieces that he carried to craft shows. Some sold, but he never really made any money at it. Then, it dawned on him that to make money he had to do it bigger and faster. That's when he decided to use the chainsaw to rough out his pieces.

One day in 1981, he carried an Indian head that he

▲ This whimsical 6' white pine fellow is called *Waving Welcome Bear.*

roughed out with a chainsaw to a show. The hair and head were left chainsaw texture, but he had spent hours chiseling out the face.

"A man came up behind me, pointing to the back of the head, and asked if that was a chainsaw carving. I told him 'yes,' and he said 'I'll take it.' He hadn't even seen the front of it! He only wanted it because it was made with a chainsaw. That was a revolutionary moment for me. I put my chisels away and from then on carved with just my chainsaw."

But the slow winter months brought more frustration. "You think you can get out there and produce, but you can't. You bundle up when you get out in the cold, and then you sweat, and your toes and fingers freeze. You try to work all wrapped up in those clothes, and you kill yourself basically. I wanted to head somewhere where I could produce during the winter months."

With family in tow, he trekked to Oregon, then traveled down the California coast, stopping to check out all the chainsaw art he could find. He pulled into a little town, whose economy was based on redwood slabs, and stopped at a shop to talk to the owner. He showed the owner his work and struck up a deal to do some production work during the winter months. Then, during the warmer months, he toured the country giving chainsaw demonstrations and entered as many shows and competitions as he could.

"I don't know how I even got up the money for the entry fees, but I did. I remember thinking in those early days that if I got $35 in a day that it was worth it. I kept my income tax returns from back then to remind me how far I've come."

The turning point

A deeply religious man, A. J. says that his faith in God saw him through the dark days. "One day I opened the Bible and was reading in Psalms. All of a sudden, I just knew that if I'd stick with it and do everything I was supposed to do that somehow I would succeed."

It was about that time that A. J. ran into Ray Murphy in the Black Hills and was so excited to see the things he could do and the patterns he produced. A visit with Jerry Ward inspired him further. "Those two guys became my mentors. They inspired me to push on to bigger and better things. That was the turning point for me. From then on, I got faster and better every year."

In fact, in the early days of chainsaw carving competitions, A. J. Lutter's speed became the stuff of legends. Feared by other artists for his ability to carve outstanding pieces fast, he placed high in all the competitions and walked away with thousands of dollars in prize money.

◄ Caught with a card up his sleeve, the *Irish Gambler* makes a speedy getaway. The piece is carved from red oak and is 4' high by 2' wide. "I like a lot of movement and flow. If the piece has motion to it, it tends to hold people's attention. So that's what I try to do."

"When I first started, it might take me two-and-a-half hours to make a two-foot-tall eagle. Later, I entered a competition where I did a seven-foot-tall banked eagle, in flight, hanging onto a rabbit, in just one hour. So yeah, I was the guy to beat at all the shows and competitions. I could hear the moans when I walked into the room. But, for me, the most important prize was the recognition and respect from other carvers."

"Come See What I Saw"

Many artists struggle, trying to find that "just right" name for their business. Not A. J. His came in a most unexpected way. "This little old lady walked up to me at a show and said, 'Come see what I saw.' I looked at her and said, 'What?' Then, she explained that her husband had owned a small sawmill by that name and told me I should use it. It's been on my business cards ever since."

Today, A. J.'s whimsical woodcarvings are in the homes of thousands of appreciative collectors, as well as in city parks, private yards, and golf courses. A significant number of these are special order pieces.

"This one lady wanted me to carve a portrait of her husband, who loved to barbeque. He had this big old chef's hat and an apron that she'd bought for him. So I did one of him dressed up like that, and they just loved it. It was supposed to go outside or in the cabin. But, oh no! It's standing right there in the living room."

A. J. was also commissioned to do a tree carving. "The guy had this big tree in his backyard, right off the deck, and he wanted something awesome in there. So I took some of the branches, and I carved them into eagles. I had an eagle banked with one wing up and one wing down. Then, I had one landing with his wings up in the air, with another one perched and several others swooping around. Into the crotch of this tree, I carved a nest with eggs. Down even further, I carved a bear crawling up the trunk. It meant moving scaffolding around quite a bit to get it done, but of course by then I was used to that, and it turned out great. The guy was absolutely flabbergasted. It was just so unbelievable to him. That was probably the most ambitious piece I've ever done."

Amazingly, this prolific carver has never had a serious injury from a chainsaw. "I've always had a proper respect for the power of that sharp saw. I've had some close calls, but I have managed to stay virtually scar free all this time," he chuckles. "However, I do seem to be falling off of scaffolding more as I age."

Those who know him understand that A. J. isn't just animated with his art. He's somewhat whimsical toward customers as well. For example, one frequently asked question is "Will the wood crack?" The standard response is to explain what precautions are taken to reduce the risk and to add that sooner or later, no matter what you do, with wood there is always that possibility.

"Well, I had one guy ask me if I guaranteed cracking. I said, 'Yes sir, I sure do. If it don't crack, you just bring it straight back to me, and I'll smack it with an ax.'"

After 25 years, his attitude toward his art remains the same. "Early on I made the decision to do nice, simple patterns that can be made fast, with a little movement and animation to them. That gives my customers the best value, and it gives me the fastest product to produce. And it's the most fun."

"I still measure myself by Norman Rockwell's standards because that's how I'd like to be known—as the 'Norman Rockwell of chainsaw carving.'"

▲ This realistic white pine *Guitar Player* strums his guitar and hollers out a tune. He stands 4' high by 3' wide.

Pat McVay

CLINTON, WASHINGTON

Pat takes a moment to sharpen his saw. Photo by Peter Wiant.

Since the artist himself is always in motion, it's no wonder that Pat McVay's carvings always look as though they'll come to life in the very next moment. "I always try to make my pieces look alive. I've seen pieces that are anatomically correct but without spirit. I try to make my pieces look like they might be moving, like they're about to turn around or take a step. It's how I challenge myself, to do complicated things. It helps me to push for aliveness in my artwork."

Some of Pat's most noted and most challenging carvings are his sports figures. "The athletes twist and turn like dancers, and to portray that in wood is difficult," Pat says. The motion he wanted to capture in his carving of Babe Ruth posed some particular challenges. "I found all these photos of Babe Ruth from different angles. I looked at where his eyes were looking, and I made his eyes looking in that direction. He had this particular swing—twisting like a corkscrew—and I made his twist with the bat behind him. I put the wrinkles in his clothing, the stripes exactly in his uniform."

Pat also carved Wayne Gretsky for a sports bar in Canada. "Wayne Gretsky came in personally and autographed the carving. This is their national hero. It was so much pressure to get him right because he's living," Pat says.

Pat was always interested in art and says that his early influences were his older brother, Mike, and his sister Judy. "They definitely influenced me to draw and do art. They were always drawing—Mike was good at cartoons, and Judy was good at horses and landscapes," Pat recalls.

Mike especially influenced Pat when it came to working wood with the chainsaw. "My older brother Mike had just returned from the 1964 New York World's Fair, where

Journal

Soon after the revelation of working with wood was floating around in my mind, I met Pat McVay. When he revealed that he was a woodcarver, I asked him if he needed help; he said, "Yes! Show up tomorrow at 9."

Pat's studio was impressive. The smell of western red cedar, the array of large unfinished carvings, the huge pile of sawdust on the ground—it was a dynamic, active, and light-hearted place, much like the man himself.

I started helping Pat by finishing up his woodcarvings. I never took a lesson from him; he had no time to give them. When he wasn't on the phone with his clients, he would race around his carvings, sawing them up. His work was interesting, and the places his commissions were going were interesting too—like Evolution of the Electric Guitar for the Hard Rock Café in Whistler, British Columbia.

In a few years, Pat gave me a brand new chainsaw with a carving bar on it. Our connection and our communication have always been about creating in wood or creating art; that is the language we speak best to each other.

—Jessie

Jesse's Memorial Chair, made of western red cedar in 2003, resides at the South Whidbey Community Park in Langley, Washington. The chair stands 5' high by 4' wide. Photo by Pat McVay.

Pat McVay

▲ This 1994, life-size carving, *The Babe*, was done in western red cedar and finished with latex paint. Commissioned by the Shark Club in Vancouver, British Columbia. Photo by Pat McVay.

he carved the front of the Oregon Pavilion and 50 totems, one for each state for the Boy Scouts. I spent summers with him in Oregon, and he would put me to work on his woodcarving—sanding, burning, and brushing. I was 15 years old. One memorable moment is when we went to a play in Portland. Mike was talking to a fellow on the steps to the playhouse. He introduced me—it was the governor of Oregon, Mark Hatfield, the guy who had hired him for the World's Fair project the year before. It gave me an idea of where art could take you."

In college, Pat studied literature, theater, and anthropology. He also took a course in art history and his interest in different artists and their artwork stuck with him. He traveled to Paris, France. "I went to visit Mike in Paris for the summer. I decided to stay. So I needed a job. Mike had a friend who was a director of the American Center for students and artists."

Henry Pillsbury, the director of the American Center in the 1970s, gave Pat a studio and a job repairing furniture for the Center's rowdy café. "Overzealous political discussions made for plenty of broken chairs and tables, so there was lots of work," Pat says.

"There was an old, dilapidated workshop that was being used for storage. The director gave me the workshop for a studio and a job to fix up all the broken furniture that was in it. I would fix all this stuff up and paint it all so it wouldn't look so bad. I used whatever paint was on hand until it was gone. Remembering Picasso's time in Paris, I joked that I had my blue period, my white period, and my red period until the red paint started to run out, too," Pat laughs.

The American Center not only provided work for Pat but also surrounded him with the art and culture of the day. Writers Gertrude Stein, Allen Ginsberg, Jean-Paul Sartre, and Henry Miller, composer John Cage, and dancer Merce Cunningham all performed at the American Center. It was a place where you could enjoy the best of American culture: film, dance, jazz, sculpture, and all of the latest artistic trends.

People at the American Center soon began asking Pat to create things as well as repair them. He would rough out his creations with a small electric chainsaw. Using hardwoods from the French countryside, he began to custom make European-style furniture.

"Mike gave me some tips and pointers and soon had this idea to go out into the French countryside, where there was a sawmill, and get some nice wood like oak, beech, and pear. He had a gas saw with him, and he showed me how to use it to incorporate a few lines of decorative motif into projects I was working on. Pretty soon I was asked if I could make furniture, and things progressed from there in my furniture and art career."

In 1973, Pat returned to the United States and lived in the rainforest of the Olympic Peninsula, where he was inspired by the works of nature around him. These ideas were incorporated into his furniture designs. "The Olympic Peninsula is a really wild area with crazy winds and all this rain. The trees that grow there twist and grow in giant, weird shapes. I still incorporate these into the work I do now. I try to use the natural shape of the wood in my pieces," Pat says.

▲ This 2002 carving
Off to School was done in
sequoia and measures 8' high by 4' wide.
Photo by Ed Sevringhaus.

▲ The town of Langley, Washington, commissioned *Two Fish on Dock*,
support pillars done in western red cedar in 2004, measuring 7' high.
Photo by Pat McVay.

◄ *Lifecycle*, in Sitka spruce, was carved for the city of Bellevue,
Washington in 2001. The carving measures 8' high and
4' wide. This piece shows the cycle of the salmon in a
continuous spiral from birth to death. Photo by Pat McVay.

▲ *Fishing Lessons*, an 8'-tall-by-5'-wide carving done in Sitka spruce, was carved in 2003 at the Oregon Divisional Chainsaw Carving Championships. Afterward, Pat took the piece home and added some finishing touches. Photo by Pat McVay.

▲ Pat's life-size *The Bluegrass Band* was carved from western red cedar and finished with latex paint. It was created in 1996 for The Hermitage in Santa Barbara, California.

Pat continued making furniture until the dawn of the 1980s, when he lost his shop. "From then on, I was a woodcarver instead of a furniture maker," Pat says. By 1981, Pat began sculpting large pieces of cedar into humorous, magical, and spirited creations, drifting further into three-dimensional woodcarving.

Now Pat McVay's special brand of woodcarved art appears in businesses and private collections along the West Coast from California to Vancouver, as well as a few other spots around the nation and world. The most notable collection of his work is his group of 200 sculptures on Pier 57 in Seattle. Many are characters depicting the era of the gold rush to Alaska. Pier 57 is a historic pier on Seattle's waterfront. The freighter *Miike Maru* docked there on August 31, 1896, and opened trade between Seattle and Japan. The following year the steamship *Portland* arrived, bearing a ton of gold from the Klondike. The ensuing gold rush would make Seattle "The Gateway to Alaska" and enrich local merchants who outfitted tens of thousands of eager prospectors.

In addition to his collections, Pat has also done a number of commission pieces. He remembers one in particular that he carved as a memorial for a teenager who was killed in a car accident. "I didn't know him personally, but everything I read about him and all the people I talked to about him said he was a cool kid. He had a cat, he loved to read, he played soccer. When he would present book reports at school, he'd bring his favorite chair and sit in it as if he was on Masterpiece Theater. When his friends came to me to make the piece, they had a drawing of the chair and the ball."

"I carved his chair with the soccer ball underneath. Then, I added his cat under the chair. The step leading up to the chair is an open book. I added a dragonfly to the back of the chair after Jesse's mother told about a day when she was missing Jesse so much. A dragonfly appeared and kept buzzing in her face. It wouldn't leave her alone until she thought that maybe it was Jesse telling her that he was okay." The chair sits in South Whidbey Community Park, overlooking the trees near the playground and soccer field where he loved to play.

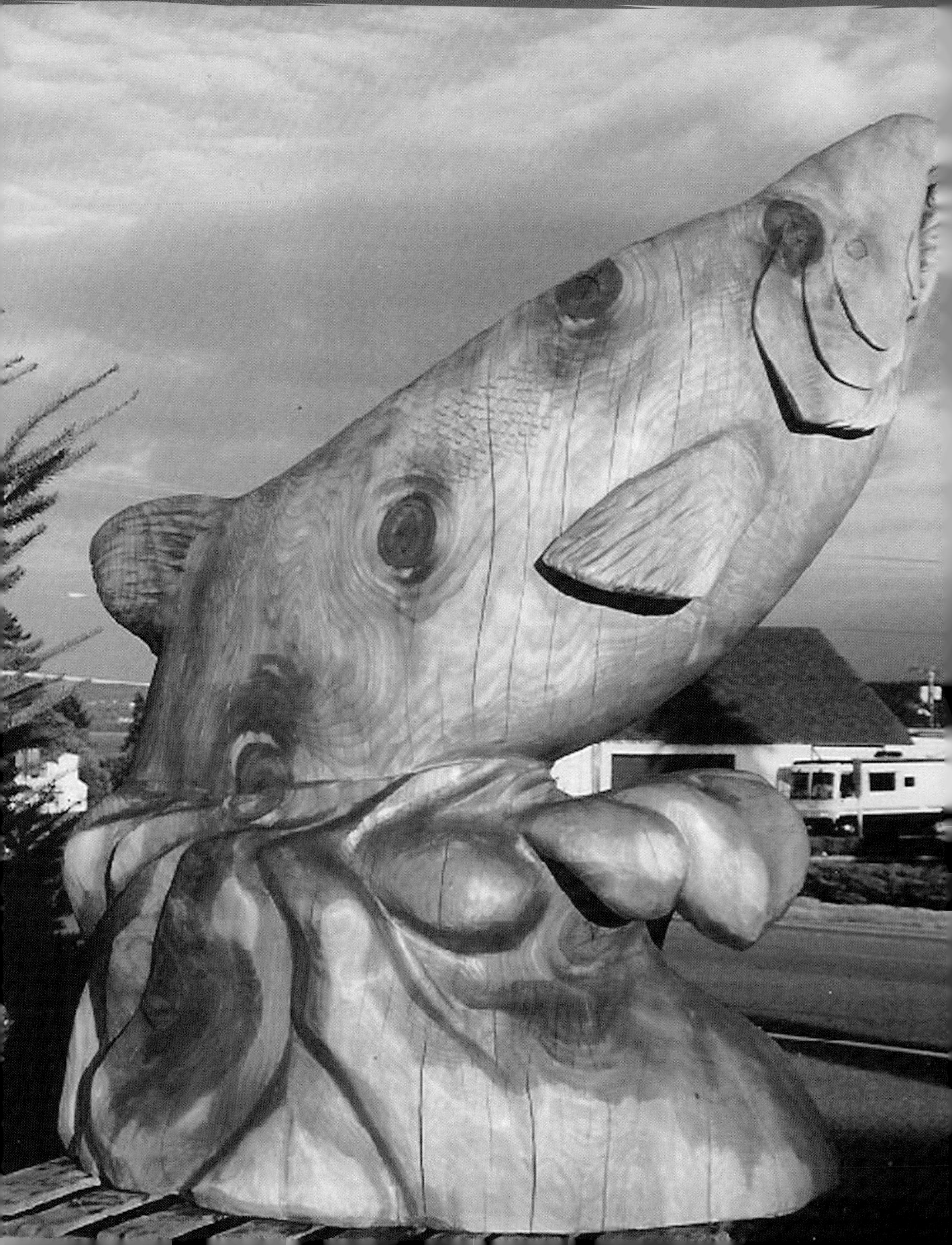

◄ This 2002 *King* is carved from Sitka spruce and stands 8' high. Carved originally at the Oregon Divisional Chainsaw Championships. Photo by Pat McVay.

▲ *Slugger*, made up of a baseball mitt, 7' tall by 4' wide; a ball in driftwood stain, 3' in diameter; and a bat, 12' long by 2½' wide. Each was carved in western red cedar in 2003.

Chainsaw carving community leader

In addition to constantly striving to better his own art, Pat also finds the time to interact with other carvers. He served as the Cascade Chainsaw Sculptors Guild President in the early 1990s and was instrumental in getting the word of chainsaw carving contests and events out to other carvers. His enthusiasm for the art form echoed in the newsletter he helped found, *The Cutting Edge*. Pat has been in many carving contests and continues to compete.

Pat encourages other carvers to compete because of what he sees as the many benefits. "Competitions are great because you have three or four days to get stuff done and a theme that pushes you in a different direction than you might have gone. Then, you take the piece home and feel like your work is stepped up a notch. It creates more of a focus for your art. And you're surrounded and inspired by all of these techniques and people."

When he's more involved in an event, as opposed to just competing in it, Pat tries to choose themes that encourage carvers to test their limits. "I try to throw something new at the carving events now. I guess that's kind of what I'm known for—always coming up with something different."

So what other advice does he have for carvers? "Get out there and do it. Approach it like a job. Just pretend like it's a contest and get going rather than saying, 'I don't feel like working today.' If I'm stuck, I try to find some part that I think will be fun or easy and focus on that. Once I've finished that part, then I'm motivated to move on to another part."

Pat is very passionate about seeing chainsaw carving receive respect as an art form. He also makes the distinction that he creates monumental sculpture and not just chainsaw art. "A lot of people stick their nose up at the chainsaw. When they think of sculpture, they have this picture of Michelangelo tapping away with his chisel. But my work impresses people who do know about sculpture."

Keeping with his philosophy of always trying new things, Pat has worked in clay, stone, concrete, steel, ice, snow, and bronze. His experimenting has also given him limitless outlets for his creativity both now and in the future. He laughs, "Maybe, when I'm too old to do chainsaw carving, I'll do clay pieces."

Steve Blanchard

SALINAS, CALIFORNIA

To see Steve Blanchard's woodcarvings, one would think he trained with a master carver and dedicated his entire life to learning the trade. But the truth of the matter is that this self-taught artist had no training at all and no obvious artistic ability—until one day when it all just clicked. The result was pure magic.

From his "bread-and-butter" bears, through a spectrum of wildlife and human figures, to benches, functional furniture, and freeform sculptures from the roots of the redwoods, there appear to be no bounds to Steve's talent. However, his latest project, the creation of a whimsical, one-of-a-kind tree house village and enchanted forest, surpassed even his wildest fantasies.

"I don't know about other carvers and how they got started. I just know what happened to me in my life," says Steve. "Everything I've ever tried has always been a struggle for me until I began to carve. I did all of these different things, but when I started carving, I immediately knew that that's who I was—a carver. It was a gift for me. I have always known that. And when you get a gift, you want to open it up to see what's in the box. That's what I've been doing ever since . . . seeing what's inside that box."

Blanchard Wood Sculpture's studio and retail outlet are located on the Pacific coast of California. Here, Steve blends his finely honed carving skill and limitless imagination to create a themed village of friendly wood spirits and crooked tree houses called "Itsyville," which has become a local tourist attraction. And if all of that were not enough, the ambitious artist has also authored a series of children's books based on the 40-foot by 40-foot village and its enchanting characters.

Both the book series and the whimsical tree house village revolve around a parallel world of wood spirits and reflect a world of imagination without boundaries as well as a little uncomplicated wisdom. "That comes from a few years of experience on the left side of the brain," he muses.

▲ Steve Blanchard perched on a bench with *Grandma*. This piece was carved at the Monterey Fair in Monterey, California, in 1995.

Journal

Steve Blanchard lives in his own world. He really does—he created a village complete with a community of little people. He has been a friend of mine for a number of years; I first met him at the Tampa, Florida Winternationals in 1992, but I didn't really get to know him until later. Though he's shy at first, he can talk, carve, and write up a storm once he opens up. He has such an endearing laugh and smile that you can't help but like the guy.

Steve truly is a gifted carver and a big thinker; he can see the big picture, but he comes through with the little picture as well.

—Jessie

◀ This tree house was delivered and installed for the customer, with additions added. The dimensions are 18½' high by 14' wide, including stairs. The tree house comfortably accommodates five adults. Photo by Steve Blanchard.

Steve Blanchard

▲ This gigantic redwood bar was carved by Steve from one huge, half-round, hollow tree trunk. The bar measures 4' high by 24' long. "I bought this huge, standing dead stump to make a tree house out of, but then I got an order from one of my customers for a bar. The stump was 8' tall, but I cut it down to four and used the top part for the other half of the bar. So it's actually two sections of one stump joined together." He sold the bar for $40,000. Photo by Steve Blanchard.

"It's all about creating an atmosphere that contrasts reality—an atmosphere where people sense some kind of magic—a timeless, defining moment. That's what I want to capture in my carvings rather than to just create something novel that people want to buy to show off to everybody, and then it's over and they have to go buy something else. I want to create an atmosphere so unique that no matter how many times they look at it, they can still sense the magic and experience the moment. See, that's like a little touch of heaven."

Twists and turns

A restless spirit, even as a child, Steve marched to the sound of a different drummer. After a stint in reform school and another in the Marines, he stumbled from one odd job to another trying to find the perfect fit. His jobs included construction, oil burner servicing, aluminum siding application, and the shrimp boat industry. Then, he became involved with a sound company out of Miami that toured with the likes of Dickie Betts, Lynard Skynard, and the Isley Brothers. With that under his belt, he ventured out to start his own sound company and promoted local music talent in Florida.

"I did this one big concert and lost everything I owned overnight—including my house!"

Steve hit the highway with only $400 in his pocket and ended up in Three Rivers, California, a small mountain town

nestled in the foothills of the Sierra Nevadas, close to Sequoia National Park. Surrounded by centuries-old sequoias, it seemed to him the perfect spot to recuperate from the financial and emotional disaster he had left behind.

After several odd jobs, Steve's entrepreneurial side surfaced again, and he built a small plant nursery, which still exists there today. But something else began to stir his restless spirit in the shadow of those giant redwoods, and, while working a landscape job one day, it all started falling into place.

"You know, I don't know what it was, but all of a sudden I just got interested in wood. My dad was a carpenter, so maybe that had something to do with it. I don't know. But, for some reason, I just kept thinking about all that redwood."

Then, a chainsaw carver came to town, cutting tree forms for tourists out of redwood chunks that seemed to call Steve's name. No stranger to a chainsaw, Steve was totally captivated by the idea, and his interest in wood was piqued even further. With the wheels of opportunity racing through his mind, he finally struck up the deal of a lifetime.

"At the time, I was having an identity crisis, and I didn't know what I wanted to do with the rest of my life. When I finally saw this guy carving, I thought, 'This is for me.' Then, I got an idea. I told him that if he would show me how to do that, I'd get him more wood. So I got some more wood, brought it back, and we started carving those little trees,"

▲ Itsyville is a whimsical village made up of seven delightful tree houses mingled with magical characters and mythical wood spirits. All of Itsyville is carved from redwood tree logs, stumps, and planks. The artist also uses paint to create contrasts. It is located outside the artist's shop in Salinas, California, where the fenced-off area of approximately 40' by 40' serves as a tourist attraction. The bear in front was carved by R. L. Blair.

▲ Large enough to accommodate real people, this tree house is made from huge chunks of redwood stumps. The stunning two-story tree house sold for $78,000 to a customer in Orinda, California. It has a spacious 8' by 8' room downstairs and an 8' by 8' room upstairs. Photo by Steve Blanchard.

recalls the artist. "Mine came out looking more like a mushroom. But I could see right away what I had done wrong and knew if I could do another one I could fix it. Then, of course, once I did that one, I had to fix that one, another one, and on and on from there until I got it right."

Soon he was selling his redwood tree carvings to the park retail store. Then one day, the storeowner asked if he could carve a bear. Without missing a beat, or ever having carved a bear, he said "yes."

"All my life I've always said 'Yes, I can do that' even if I had never actually done it before because I always believed that I would be able to," he explains. "From that point on, everything I saw I started to carve in my head automatically. I mean I would catch myself doing it. It was just like magic to me, and it's still that way. Everything I look at I carve in my head."

It turned out Steve was right. He could carve adorable bears that sold quickly. Then, he found he could also make eagles, Indians, benches, dolphins, seals, angels, and human figures.

Steve Blanchard

▲ A closeup of *Christ's Promised Return* shows the fine details of one of the angels. Photo by Steve Blanchard.

◄ *Christ's Promised Return.* Artist statement: "A 2000-year-old redwood was perhaps the perfect medium for this timeless subject. It is possible that on the very day Christ recited his promise, the seed of this redwood gave birth to its own. Tried by the elements of time, it stood for a season, as a testament to one much greater, that which held the promise of eternal life. Ironically, it was from its own death, while its fractured, lifeless body lay hopelessly on the forest floor, that the voice of destiny would call one that had, until then, slept silently in the mind of the sculptor." Carved in ancient growth redwood, in three main pieces, it stands 11' tall, 10' wide, and 5' deep and is finished with natural oil.

The root of his art

Eventually Steve left the little town with a truckload of carvings. He landed in Monterey, where he further honed his skills at the Burlwood Galleries, a well-known carving and redwood furniture store owned by Marilyn Buck who, incidentally, became the "love of his life." There he learned a very important lesson destined to become the root of his art.

"I worked next to a Vietnamese carver who blocked everything out and measured everything he did. I said to myself, 'I'm not going to do that. I'm going to force myself to use my imagination and just picture these things in my mind.' And so I did. I never even used reference books either. I would just force myself to come up with stuff."

After a period of those self-imposed mental exercises, Steve realized that it was probably okay to use references, that they might enhance his imagination.

"So I would find detailed pictures of things and try to get as close to realistic as I could. But, over time, I realized that the closer you get to realism, the more your mistakes become evident. So I kind of backed off on that and tried instead to give everything a little bit of character, and it seemed to work for me."

Today this artist relies on his mental drawing board, picturing the piece in his mind before he actually starts carving.

"I have always done that since the very beginning. Eventually, I got to the point where I could project the whole carving and figure out all the problems that might develop before I ever started up the chainsaw. I don't think that's altogether unique either. I have talked to other carvers who have developed the same process."

"The downside of that is that it gets boring for me because I've already carved the piece in my head before I ever pick up a saw. So, for me, the challenge keeps changing. Before, it was 'Can I carve a bear?' or 'Can I carve this?' or 'Can I carve that?' Then, when I got this retail store, the challenge became survival because it costs money to have a business. At first, I did a lot of custom orders. But then the challenge became carving what I wanted to carve and still making a living at it. It was a real struggle because I had to know what sells and what works to keep my business going. Then, this whole village thing developed and that became the challenge. It was something that I couldn't see the end of. To this day, I still can't see the end of it, so I just keep adding to it."

In the early to mid-1990s, Steve tried the show and chainsaw competition circuit and did very well. Soon, he began to see the many differences between what he did and what other chainsaw carvers did and no longer felt like he fit in. The chasm widened until Steve fell through the cracks and dropped out of competition.

"I've always used a chainsaw, but I never really thought of myself as a chainsaw carver. I'm more of a woodcarver that uses a chainsaw along with all kinds of power tools, grinders, sanders, finishing tools, and anything else to get the job done. Everybody has different opinions about that. Some use the finishing tools and some don't. Even in the competitions they have differences of opinion, so I just kind of dropped out and did my own thing."

Steve started off using small redwood blocks and limbs for his carvings. Now, this artist prefers huge chunks, stumps, and gnarled and twisted tree roots, which he transforms into beautiful works of art.

"Early on, I discovered that when they clear the land up in the Crescent City area in Northern California, they leave big piles of these trunks and roots. Some of them have been just lying there for 20 years. So I buy a truckload of roots at a time to make benches and tree houses and stuff like that out of them. To me, that's the nicest part of the tree. I don't use hardly anything else anymore but roots."

Art, like life, is self-perpetuating. Constantly changing and evolving, it drives Steve to explore the bold new worlds of his creativity. Still, even Steve admits that it was a big stretch of the imagination to get from bears to tree houses.

"Actually, I was just starting a new carving when another carver stopped by to visit. With the first cut, I hit rot in the wood. Knowing I wouldn't get far with that sculpture, I was about to cut it up and use it for something else. The other carver laughed and said half-jokingly, 'You ought to just make a tree house out of it.' So it ended up that I did just that, and he worked on it with me. I liked it so much that I wanted to see more of them around my shop, plus I thought I could use them as a display to catch people's attention and get them to stop. This turned out to be the perfect thing, and it all sort of grew from there."

Today, many of Steve's extravagant, one-of-a-kind tree houses stand two stories high with rooms large enough to accommodate five adults. One of his more recent tree houses sold for an incredible $78,000.

"I'm very fortunate to have something to do like this. I'm challenged continually. Not that there isn't a lot of suffering that goes with it. But that's okay because in order to experience the greatest highs, you have to experience the greatest lows. Otherwise you can't appreciate it."

"Bottom line with me—it still seems to whittle down to atmosphere. It's about contrasting the images that the world projects with a moment of timelessness and seeing how long I can sustain that for me . . . and anyone else who cares to take a peek."

▲ A life-size W. C. Fields, also in redwood, attracts a lot of attention at the Monterey County Fairgrounds. "I carved at the fair a week at a time for four years. We'd bring in big chunks of wood and carve them." Photo by Pat McVay.

Ben Risney

SPRING CITY, PENNSYLVANIA

While many chainsaw carvers gradually chip and buzz their way to the top, Ben Risney entered the frontier with a flash and rode a fiery trail to chainsaw stardom at the age of only twenty-five. Today, he draws hundreds of people to his shows, astounding them with his speed, agility, and awe-inspiring artistic ability. He also wows them with his showmanship.

"Sometimes I'll interact a little bit with the people. Like I'll shoot chips 25 feet up into the air that spray down on them, or I'll twirl the saw like a butcher twirls his knife and other moves I've come up with to let people know that, hey, I'm not just some weekend carver."

"Speed is important to me. When I start a project, I pretty much want to get it done in a day. That's the fun for me—the immediacy of it all. That's why I switched over from handcarving to chainsaw carving. For the shows, I make the nicest thing I can in a 45-minute session," says Ben.

Speed, power, excitement, and showmanship—all of these factors contribute to his crowd-pleasing performances. The carver spends four months each year on the road performing at fairs, openings, and other entertainment venues. At the end of his travel circuit, he returns to his home in Pennsylvania to further refine his art, design new carvings, and work on his many commission pieces.

Ben's shows are booked through Masters of the Chainsaw—a booking company exclusively for chainsaw carvers. As one of their star performers, he has crisscrossed the country many times over. According to the artist, his most exciting trip was to Japan in 2001.

"What a great way to see Japan! It was wonderful to be

▲ Ben in action at a fair. Photo by Jen Ruth.

Journal

When I met Ben, I was struck by his humble and modest personality; however, when he performs, he dazzles the crowds with speed, accuracy, good artistry, and high energy. Other carvers frequently emulate Ben's inventive, original chainsaw woodcarving designs for his 45-minute shows. Ben is able to put 100 percent into his performance art show by understanding the mechanisms of the chainsaw, the cuts it makes, and the anatomy of his subject matter.

—Jessie

◄ *Stump Carving* was carved into a dead maple tree in the yard of a local federal judge. "He turned out kind of neat looking with all the hair blowing around and all. His nose is a little funky because I hit a big knot. But I did some things and worked around it." Photo by Ben Risney.

Ben Risney

there and to perform and teach what I do to a totally different culture. They were fascinated by it. There were three of us putting on a mini contest, and as soon as we shut the saws off, they rushed the stage just like at a Garth Brooks concert! People don't respond like that at our shows in the States. They're much more reserved. But that was something I'll never forget."

Instantaneous success

Off-stage, Ben is humble, modest, completely unassuming, and truly amazed by his own success. However, none of this came as a surprise to those who knew him growing up. In fact, they would probably say he was destined to do something just like this. He attributes youth and dexterity for his quick rise to fame, but others say it's true grit mixed with natural talent.

"I came from a kind of crafty lineage. My parents are both artists, and we always designed and built whatever we needed. So I never thought my talent was anything special or unusual. I just picked up stuff really quickly when it came

to wood. In school, I could build a gun cabinet in 12 hours where it would take the other kids 50 or 60 hours."

A defining point in Ben's life came in grade school when students were assigned to draw a map of Texas for homework.

"I cut one out of plywood with a jigsaw and got a marker and drew in all the different things like the capital and the logging regions and stuff like that. When I brought it into class, the teacher freaked out and gave me triple A-pluses. She made such a big deal out of it, but I only did it because I didn't have any poster board," he laughs.

After high school, he worked as a general contractor; later he got into cabinetry. "Actually, I am a fourth-generation cabinetmaker and carpenter."

In 1994, Ben picked up a chainsaw to carve his first piece of art. "My uncle was a recreational chainsaw carver. He carved this big old bear head out of a log and hung it on the wall of his house in the mountains. I was just fascinated by it, and I decided to make a bear of my own," he explains.

The sawdust had barely settled on his first piece before it was sold. The same thing happened with his second carv-

◀ ▲ Ben's 45-minute, high-energy chainsaw art performances draw huge crowds and enthrall spectators. Photos courtesy Ben Risney.

▲ A bear emerges from a white pine tree, guided by the skillful hands of Ben Risney. The chainsaw artist pauses briefly to etch out the bear's nostrils. Photo courtesy Ben Risney.

ing. "Then my third piece was like a $1,500 commission. I thought, 'Wow! This is a great way to make a living!'" His success was instantaneous.

"Chainsaw carving is a lot of hard work; even if you have a lot of raw talent, you can never substitute behind-the-saw experiences. I admire anyone that has a real strong work ethic and gets out there and carves."

Flair for the unusual

Eleven years into the game, Ben has developed non-traditional techniques that others are beginning to emulate. "I don't carve like most artists. That probably comes from the fact that I am completely self-taught. I had never really even seen anyone carve chainsaw art. I just did what was comfortable," he says.

"The chainsaw is an awkward thing. It's not meant for carving. So I kind of modify things. Whatever I have to do to get the right effect while I'm carving, that's what I'll do. If I've got to flip the saw inside out and upside down to get my bar in there and clean something out, that's what I do.

I've chopped some things off saws to make that easier, like parts of the handles and guards—stuff you're not supposed to remove—so I can get more maneuverability. Whatever way I can manipulate that bar to get in there efficiently, that's how it's done."

Another unusual technique of Ben's, when he's not doing a show, is to wear a headset and listen to music while he carves. "Carving is a very singular occupation. You go off by yourself and do your own thing. The music helps relax me and gives me a little bit of a beat to carve to, and that helps. It gets really boring when you're carving all day long by yourself with no other interaction. It's also good because it blocks out all other distractions."

Although his carvings come in all shapes and sizes, Ben says he prefers to do smaller pieces of two to three feet. "I like to do something that'll fit in the truck or a car—something that the average person can stick under their arm and walk away with. Some of my pieces are really delicate because I'll try all kinds of things to keep them from looking like just a hunk of wood—like carving pencil-thin legs on a heron."

This red fox, 15' long by 5' wide, was carved in red oak and is one of Ben's more unusual commissions. It is the first in a series of 27 horse jumps used at the Radnor Hunt International Three-Day Event in Malvern, Pennsylvania. Ben was commissioned to carve one jump each year. "So I guess I'll be doing that for the next 26 years," he laughs. "Next year I plan to carve a big alligator water jump down there." Photo courtesy Ben Risney.

A proud 8'-tall elk carved from tulip poplar was a commissioned piece for an avid elk hunter. "He always wanted to get something that big, so I made him one," Ben laughs. "I always work kind of loose with a commission. They've got to leave it up to me. I'm a pain like that." Photo courtesy Ben Risney.

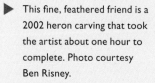 This fine, feathered friend is a 2002 heron carving that took the artist about one hour to complete. Photo courtesy Ben Risney.

You've got to be really daring or really stupid to do that, I'm not sure which. But I stay with the smaller pieces because, in general, they hold together pretty well."

Texture is very important to Ben. He'll spend precious minutes at a show just shaving the carving with the bar of the saw. At home he uses hydraulic chainsaws.

"I can't use them at a show because they run off heavy compressors. But the benefits of hydraulic saws are that they're quieter and there are no fumes, so you can carve indoors. They don't have a centrifugal clutch—it's a central drive—so it leaves a nice, clean cut every time. Technically, you can even sand with it. For example, if you are carving on a dolphin, it leaves a nice, smooth finish, whereas a regular gas chainsaw, with that centrifugal clutch, leaves chatter lines."

This artist says he prefers poplar and pinewood for his carvings because they are both soft, bright woods that show off the details of the piece, whereas darker woods tend to hide them.

He never works from a sketch. Rather, he draws his ideas and inspiration from flipping through art and literature books. Then he develops and adapts those images in his mind until he has a clear picture of what he wants to do. He cautions, however, that how the piece looks in his mind and how the actual carving turns out may not be exactly the same.

"With wood you just never know what you might run into. There might be a knot in the wrong place or a hollow spot or a nail or something else that you can't work around. So you have to be really careful about how much wood you take away during the beginning stages of carving and learn to adapt."

Ben lives on a five-acre farm, about 45 minutes from Philadelphia, where he has several horses. In his free time, he enjoys horseback riding and roping. He operates Ben Risney Woodcarving out of a barn in the winter and outdoors during warmer weather. "I guess an artist is supposed to call it a studio, but I just call it my barn," he laughs.

At only 35 years of age, with more than a decade of experience under his belt, this carver is not entertaining thoughts of giving it up anytime soon. He does, however, concede that the older he gets, the more he appreciates his senior carvers.

"I'm still fairly young, but I can definitely see a difference between being 20 and being 35 in my back and joints from carving all day long. I am amazed at guys in their fifties or older that have done it for a long time and are still doing it. I don't know how they're holding up because I'm already starting to feel pains and strains," he chuckles.

"A lot of people say it's like you're a professional athlete, and you only have so many carvings in your back, and at some point you're going to have to find a real job. I think about that in the back of my head, but I hope it's not true. I feel very fortunate and very blessed to be able to do what I'm doing. I'll never forget where I came from and how I got here, and all the people who supported me along the way."

▲ This 3'-tall *Horse Head*, replete with lifelike details, was carved at a fair in 2004. Photo by Ben Risney.

Dennis Roghair

HINCKLEY, MINNESOTA

Mountain lions pouncing on prey, eagles soaring through the air, wolves howling on the mountaintop—these are but a few of the dramatic chainsaw carvings of Dennis Roghair. Born from his love of wildlife, his true-to-life carvings also include poignant portraits that capture the essence of human life.

Among the early names in chainsaw carving, Dennis hit the competition circuit in the 1980s, winning several world competitions. Audiences were captivated with his flair for the unusual and his innate ability to evoke emotion through his carvings.

"I believe my woodcarving ability is a God-given talent. I think at the time of my birth, God looked down on me and said, 'This guy is going to really need some help, so I'll make him a carver.' God creates the creator, and it's an amazing thing," says the artist. "But I'm not perfect. There is always room for improvement. I look back at some of the carvings I did thirty years ago, and I don't even want to tell anybody I did them. Good art is always evolving. Even in some of the things I do now, I can see what I should do differently next time."

Dennis's studio and gift shop, called the Kettle River Carving Company, is located in Hinckley, Minnesota. Visitors walking through the front door of his shop are most often greeted by Dennis himself, standing on the scaffolding, working on his latest carving. "People come in here to watch me now all the time. It's kind of a draw to the store," he laughs. Out behind the studio area is a nice, quiet gift shop featuring Dennis's carvings.

Retired now from the show and competition circuit, this artist only travels to do commission pieces. His most ambitious project is at the Minnesota State Fairgrounds in Minneapolis. Having suffered a devastating loss of trees due

▲ Dennis Roghair's signature

◄ Dennis and his carving, *Mountain Lion and Bighorn Sheep*, in white pine. The carving is 12½' tall.

Journal

Dennis is somewhat of a legend among other carvers. I've never heard another carver say a bad thing about him. They all talk about him with awe and reverence.

Speaking with Dennis is an engaging thing. I felt like he was studying and observing, even while he was talking; maybe that is why his carvings of people and animals are so good. He takes it all in, memorizing the details and studying emotions and movements. When the moment arrives to carve, he has it all figured out.

—Jessie

◄ *Voyager* is located at River Side Park in Pine City, Minnesota, and is carved in redwood from Northern California. The total length of the log is 40'. Some of it is buried for stability. The size of the man is 26½' tall, and the base is 6'. The widest point is at his shoulders, which is 8'. It is Dennis's largest carving.

Dennis Roghair

▲ *Guardian Angel* was carved into a 10' white pine log. Her wings were added later.

to Dutch elm disease, officials hired Dennis and other artists to breathe new life into dead trees throughout the fairground. They transformed the remaining trunks into works of art. The project spanned a ten-year period with Dennis creating 27 of the 40 magnificent carvings now located on the grounds. His work is also found on the grounds of the governor's mansion in St. Paul, Minnesota.

"There was a tree in the yard area, and they wanted a carving. So I cut up the tree, and from the bottom piece I carved a little girl in a garden with a watering can. She's watering the flowers in the garden area. Out of the upper section of the tree I carved a little boy holding flowers behind his back."

Love of wildlife turns to art

Dennis Roghair grew up in a little town in northwest Iowa called Alton. At four years old, the boy's parents gave him a small pocketknife, and he started whittling his first little woodland creatures. By the time his teen years rolled around, he had acquired mallets, chisels, and gouges as well and produced even more refined wildlife likenesses. But despite taking all of the available art classes in high school, he admits that he never did master the art of drawing or painting.

"My wife has seen some of my drawings, and she told me that if anybody asked me if I could draw, I should tell them 'no' because if they see my drawings, they'll think I can't carve either!"

Dennis's love of wildlife spurred him on to college where he majored in wildlife management at Utah State University. In fact, he paid his way though college by selling his wildlife artwork.

"I was still doing handcarving, mostly wildlife reliefs, plus anything else I could do to get money. It was a big college, and a lot of the professors bought the stuff that I was doing. Some of them even paid me to go to their homes or cabins to carve doors and mantles and things like that for them."

During this time, he not only sold his pieces but also actually got paid to teach carving classes through community education courses. In 1973, Dennis stumbled upon Kent Peterson, a carver from Logan, Utah, who was doing some work with a chainsaw.

"He was the first guy I ever saw doing chainsaw art. I later looked him up, and he gave me pointers on how to do it. I thought that was a good way to get rid of excess wood on handcarvings. So I traded a black powder rifle with a hand-carved stock for my first chainsaw."

In his last semester, Dennis learned that students majoring in wildlife management were required to take a course that taught them how to write a resume. The grade for that class was based on the resume. After the first class period, the teacher asked Dennis what kind of wildlife management he was interested in.

▲ *From His Bounty*, a 1991 carving in Dutch elm, silently gives thanks for nature's bounty at the entrance to the food court on the Minnesota State Fairgrounds.

"I told him that I didn't plan on going into the management field because I didn't want to sit behind a desk doing paperwork. I told him I wanted to be a woodcarver. Then, as a joke, I suggested he just let me turn in a woodcarving for my resume. He said, 'Sure, bring it to the next class.' Well, I had just finished a mountain lion, so the next class found me with a three-foot-long mountain lion laying on my lap, feeling somewhat foolish. The instructor called me up to the front of the room, mountain lion in tow. He held the lion up and said, 'Dennis wants to be a woodcarver. This is his resume, and he has an A.' To me he said, 'Dennis, you don't have to come back to class.'"

While still in school, Dennis married. After graduation, he took a job in Minnesota as a counselor working with emotionally disturbed youth. He did that for five years, carving all the while. Then, in 1979, he made the momentous decision to charge headlong into chainsaw carving full-time.

▲ This life-size *Voyager* stands with paddle in hand in the city of Plymouth, Minnesota. He depicts the late 1700s era in that region.

Dennis Roghair

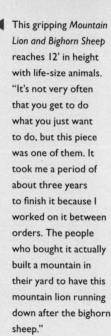

This gripping *Mountain Lion and Bighorn Sheep* reaches 12' in height with life-size animals. "It's not very often that you get to do what you just want to do, but this piece was one of them. It took me a period of about three years to finish it because I worked on it between orders. The people who bought it actually built a mountain in their yard to have this mountain lion running down after the bighorn sheep."

"I knew that I had made enough money carving to pay for college, but I didn't know if I could make enough to take care of my family. I had just gotten a big order that would bring in enough money to take care of things for a while. So, I quit my job and started on that order. When it was done, the guy told me that he'd had a financial setback and couldn't buy it. I didn't have any idea what to do, but two days later some money came in the mail anonymously—just enough to see us through."

Today, as a highly successful chainsaw carver, Dennis has authored his first book with fellow carver, Jamie Doeren, of Wisconsin, entitled *Chainsaw Carving an Eagle*. Why eagles?

"When you do chainsaw carving, you learn real quick that the most popular item is a bear. Everybody does bears because everybody wants bears. So, to be successful as a chainsaw carver, you have to do bears. The next most popular thing is eagles."

Dennis's favorite wood for chainsaw sculpting is white pine because it is soft enough that it can be carved easily and hard enough that it holds the details. "Catalpa is my second choice. It's not as abundant here, so I don't get it very often, but the grain in it is very dramatic. It's a really neat wood."

From inspiration to creation

For all his quick wit and great sense of humor, when it comes to art, Dennis strives for realism. "I try to achieve realism—something lifelike. I've had all kinds of opportunities to see animals up close and study the things they do. I try to capture that in the most lifelike carving possible."

Last summer, Dennis received an order for a raccoon. The day he was to carve it, he happened to spy a dead raccoon on the side of the road. Thinking it would make good reference material, he scooped it up and carried it back to the studio.

"It was freshly dead, so it wasn't like it was nasty or anything. I just kind of propped it up into the position I planned for the carving. When I was all done, I looked at it and thought, 'Man, something looks wrong with that carving'. I called my wife in for her opinion because she's always honest with me. She took one look and said, 'It looks dead!' And she was right. It did look dead, because it was dead," he laughs. So, he buried the thing and started over.

Like most people of a creative nature, ideas come easy to this carver. It could be that something he observed in the wild sparks his imagination, or perhaps something somebody says might strike up an idea. Surprisingly, it might even be a mistake that stirs the mind into action.

"I could be trying to do a certain thing on a piece and make a mistake, because with a chainsaw you can make mistakes really fast if you're not careful. But sometimes those mistakes force you to change the carving, and it turns out even better than your original idea. It happens."

However, Dennis points out that the creative juices may not always flow full force. Sometimes an idea only trickles out; other times, he might even draw a complete blank. Then there are those occasions when an idea jumps into his head just in the nick of time. Those ideas, he suggests, might even be the best.

"I remember the second world competition that I was in. We were supposed to do a scene with multiple aspects to it and, of course, we were being judged. There I was, standing with scaffolding all around and hundreds of people watching when they said, "Go!" And I thought, "Okay, what am I going to do?" I had no idea! My mind just went completely blank. After a few moments, I thought of an eagle, so I did one of those. Then, I thought of having the eagle flying over

▲ Life-size *Lamplighter* pauses briefly to lean against the lamppost and light his pipe. "That piece we wired so that there is a little light in his hand that lights up his face. He is in Roseville, a suburb of Minneapolis."

the tops of some trees, so I did that. Then I thought of some rocks, and then an Apache underneath them in front of a cave. The ideas just came to me one at a time. And, when I was about halfway done, the title came to me too—Silent Sentries. That was the first world competition that I won."

The one thing Dennis has no patience for is repetition. "I don't like doing the same thing over and over. I tried a production piece one summer. Someone wanted me to carve a little bear cub. When I got done, I thought it was so neat that I made another one, and another. As fast as I could make them that summer, they sold. I think I did 200 of those things. After that I said, 'That's it—I'm not doing any more production pieces. One-of-a-kinds are what I do now.' Occasionally I'll do another one of those little bears,"

he chuckles. "But I have so many ideas that I just don't have time to do them all, and that's what keeps this interesting."

There are many methods and techniques involved in chain-saw carving, and each artist develops the ones that work best for him or her. "Typically, what I do on a carving, which is kind of different from a lot of people, is carve the head first. I don't even rough out the rest of it. I'll usually just do the head. The head is the hardest thing to do. If you get a really good head and screw everything else up, you've still got a bust out of it. But if you block everything else in and then screw up the head, you've pretty much lost the whole chunk of wood."

What does Dennis Roghair do for fun? "Carving is my fun. If I didn't have to do this for work, I would still be carving. It's what I love to do."

Equestrian. This proud 15-foot Englishman, carved in oak, is a commission piece with an unusual story. "My clients had this huge, dead oak tree that the tree people said had to come down. Their son was going to get married in two weeks, so they decided to wait until after the reception to take the tree down. A couple of days later a storm blew in. The son was just leaving in his little M.G. convertible when his mom saw him leave. She hollered out the window to tell him not to forget something. Well, he hit the brakes to hear what she was saying, and right at that moment the tree came crashing down across the drive right in front of his car. It would have crushed him if she hadn't stopped him. It was just a miraculous happening."

▶ *State Fair Heritage*, a carved collage of important state fair historical events, was carved in 1998 out of the oldest tree at the Minnesota State Fairgrounds. "It depicts Teddy Roosevelt hanging onto a stick because that is where he gave his famous speech, 'Speak Softly but Carry a Big Stick.' Then, there is a hot air balloon because they had hot air balloon races there also. And there are locomotives crashing into each other because that's something else they used to do at state fairs."

THE BALLOON FAIR 1857

MINNESOTA STATE FAIR

Brian J. Ruth

LEHIGHTON, PENNSYLVANIA

When performance chainsaw carver Brian J. Ruth gets out there to razzle-dazzle a crowd, it's not just the wood chips that fly—you can see sparks flying too as this gregarious showman connects with his astounded audience. Through his power-packed, people-pleasing, high-performance chainsaw demonstrations, he has carved out a niche for himself and other carvers in the show and fair circuits.

His legendary antics during the 45-minute performances have proved highly effective in helping to promote chainsaw carving and have generated increased interest in the art, both at home and abroad. In fact, Brian J. Ruth has left a trail of sawdust halfway around the globe.

"The thing for me is speed. I like to get a piece done and get it done quickly while keeping it interesting as a show for people. To do that, you have to keep moving, and you can't even slow down long enough to really look at the piece. There's no time to think. The saw's got to be in the wood the whole time, and sawdust has to be continually coming off that piece of wood. Otherwise, people will lose interest," attests the carver.

"As long as it keeps changing shape and keeps developing, it'll hold the audience. But as soon as you slow down to do the details, people lose interest because they can already see a bear with a fish in its mouth. It's already there, and they really don't care to see you put in all the fur. I mean, you can detail a piece for days, but, at these shows, you've got to quit when you start to lose their interest. So the trick is to make a nice piece with just enough detail really, really fast."

◀ Brian teaches his son, Zack, how to handle a chainsaw. Photo by Jen Ruth.

Journal

Brian J. Ruth has established himself as one of the best performance chainsaw carvers in the world. His performances are like watching a ballet. His precise moves, his well-thought-out designs, and his love for what he does is a joy to watch. Brian spent many years carving solely for the purpose of performance, often in an hour or less. But he doesn't limit himself to expression in just one way—he has been known to create art on a large scale, throwing out the limitations of time, leading to more detailed, creative, and expressive pieces of art.

—Jessie

◀ Carved in maple, *Dragonfly* is 6' high and 6' in diameter. The wings are added on. This was carved at the Chainsaw Carver's Rendezvous in Ridgway, Pennsylvania. "I did this using the shape of the crotch of the tree to make the body of the dragonfly. To make the wings, I carved one big, fat wing and cut the holes in it while it was still strong, then split it in half."

Brian J. Ruth

▲ Brian J. Ruth at home in 2004, carving a chunk of Tennessee cedar. In this series of photos, you can actually see the various stages as this large hummingbird carving evolves.

In 1992, Brian J. Ruth founded Masters of the Chainsaw, a booking company for professional chainsaw carvers that has been instrumental in promoting the art and filling the demand for carvers at special events. To date, the organization has placed 60 carvers at nearly 1600 events, such as fairs, festivals, grand openings, hardware stores, and other venues in almost every state in the U.S. as well as in Canada and Japan.

In 2001, he turned operations of Masters of the Chainsaw over to his very capable, equally enthusiastic wife, Jen, freeing him from the business aspect and allowing him more time to concentrate on his art. Brian also conducts a chainsaw carving school in Toei, Japan, where he has taught over 100 people to master the art of chainsaw carving. He even initiated a chapter of Masters of the Chainsaw in Japan to help Japanese chainsaw carvers get started and to further promote the art throughout that country.

"It's been a great experience. Especially teaching the beginners class. It's so exciting just to see the look on the students' faces when they accomplished their first carving. It's a really neat feeling."

Work in progress

Brian J. Ruth, born on an Air Force base in Suffolk, England, was raised in Montgomery County, Pennsylvania. Although he graduated from Villanova University with a Bachelor of Science degree in business administration, his penchant for art blossomed early, as evidenced by his dedication to learning oil painting as a child.

"In fifth grade, a friend and I bought canvases and oil paints and books, and we used to go home after school and do oil paintings. But I never was really good with color. I'm better at sketching things. I can reproduce what I see, and I'm real good with the spatial relations thing."

But the road from brushes to chainsaws took an unusual turn. During college, he went to work for a tree service as a climber. Then, one day in 1979, while visiting a craft show at a local mall, he spied some art made by local carver Stev Mohr, who was working with an electric chainsaw behind a Plexiglas enclosure. He was intrigued by the work. A few days later, he took his climbing saw with a standard 14-inch bar and a piece of wood and carved his first owl.

▲ Brian J. Ruth at the New York State Fair, working on another 45-minute showpiece. This white pine log eventually morphs into a frog perched on a log with a planter inserted on the side. Show pieces usually auction off at anywhere from $300 to $2,300. Photo by Jen Ruth.

▶ Tree frogs are a favorite subject for this artist. This one, carved from white pine, was a gift for his wife. It stands 3' high. "This was a lot more complicated than the ones I do at the 45-minute shows."

"At the time, I was doing tree work with a chainsaw—you know, climbing up trees, dangling from a rope where I really couldn't make a mistake. I got to be real good with the feel and the cut of the saw. I had blocked out some tables and chairs too, using straight cuts, but I'd never actually shaped anything. I didn't think it would be a monumental task though, so I tried it."

"Then I thanked my dad for the education and announced I was going to be a chainsaw carver," he laughs.

From that point on, the chainsaw was buzzing. Brian got himself an agent and was off. Since indoor work required the use of an electric chainsaw, he used small-diameter wood for his 45-minute shows. Working on such a small scale allowed him to add more detail and further refine his skills.

"When I first started carving with the chainsaw, I decided I had to make things realistic—it proved that I could get the end result that I wanted with a chainsaw. You know, if you do an abstract with a chainsaw, nobody knows if it turned out the way you meant for it to. I wanted to do things where I could prove that I could make what I wanted to make. So that's why I started with realistic work, and because I love wildlife, my carvings leaned towards that."

Brian J. Ruth

▲ Brian J. Ruth impresses a crowd in Japan with an energy-packed chainsaw carving performance. Photo by KG Kidokoro.

By 1984, he decided to take over his own management and put his business degree to work. "Stuff I learned in school came in handy, such as promoting, marketing, and providing press releases. I came up with the name 'Master of the Chainsaw.' I figured I wasn't a master yet, but I thought that having a name like that would inspire me and make me live up to it. So I did my best and hoped that nobody who could carve better than me came around," he chuckles.

Initially, it was just Brian, but the demands for demonstration art exceeded what he could produce. So he called up Dennis Beach and passed on some shows to him. Then, in 1990, as the mall business began to slowly die out because of a change in marketing strategies, Brian moved into the festival arena.

"I found that there was an unbelievable demand for carving shows at fairs and decided to start representing other carvers professionally, too. I just tacked an *s* onto Master, and now a bunch of guys have to live up to it!"

During his very first year of competition, Brian won two first-place awards at the Winter Nationals in Tampa, Florida, in 1991. "The wood was bigger than what I was used to using at those mall shows, but what I did was basically line up a few small subjects on top of each other, creating a scene in one larger carving."

Today Brian's showpieces generally run in the three-to-four-foot range. However, non-show pieces and commission works run the creative gamut with no size restrictions. They range from tiny, one-inch miniature animals to giant, 14-foot human figures, all done with various chainsaws.

"I started wondering how small a figure I could do, so I began making a handful of little, one-inch carvings of animals that you could easily tell what they were—bears, eagles, giraffes, elephants—and they were totally done with a chainsaw with a standard bar. I just was able to get a lot of control with the tip of the saw. I could make dust come off it instead of chips. I've carved fish so thin that if you held them up, you could see some light come through them. So, when I

▲ These various carvings were all done in black walnut. They stand approximately 16" to 20" high and were carved in the early 1980s. All of them were done with a 14' electric saw with a standard bar. Photos courtesy Brian J. Ruth.

ended up blowing up to bigger carvings and using gas saws, I was able to do ¹/₁₆ and ¹/₃₂ of an inch tolerance detail."

"I'd be bored stiff if I did the same thing all the time, so I'm always creating new pieces and reworking the old designs. As I get better and faster, I add more detail to them, or I'll add a whole second wolf head to the piece or something like that so it's always progressing. Even at shows where I've gone back for 15 or 20 years, the work has continued to change and get better. I figure I'm going to be really good someday, and then you'd better watch out!"

A collection of Brian J. Ruth's works can be seen at the Iowa State Fair where, in 1998, he transformed the stumps of storm-damaged trees into poignant works of art. Using fairgoers as models, his carvings portray different ages, ranging from children to grandparents.

"These were people I'd actually seen at the fair. When the fair officials picked up on that, they started auctioning off the rights to model for the carvings as a fundraising event. So, for a couple thousand dollars, you could have your grandmother model for one of the carvings permanently on display at the fair, which was kind of neat."

Brian's work can also be viewed at the Kittery Trading Post in Kittery, Maine, where he has done a piece for their event each year for 20 years running. Some of the pieces are as large as 14 feet tall. When the post started running out of

room, Brian began turning out elaborate signs and benches.

Does he ever run out of ideas? Well, you would never know it to watch him, but Brian says that he has stood a log up under watchful eyes a ton of times not knowing exactly what he was going to make.

"I'll make a quick decision as I'm walking around the log looking at it like I'm waiting for it to speak to me or something," he laughs. "A lot of times the wood does have a certain shape to it or character that you try to use to enhance your carving. But, most of the time, it's just a round log twice as tall as it is wide, and you've got to be able to pull a whole lot of different stuff out of it. I know I can always just stick a bear head in and figure out something else as I go along. But yes, with the hundreds and hundreds of different designs that I do, it's amazing that I could run out of ideas or not be able to come up with something in my head that I can do or want to do, but it happens."

Does he ever surprise himself? "Yes. When I'm really pushed, I'll kind of push a design and it keeps getting better and better. I wonder sometimes where all this is going to go . . . and why can't I be there already," he jokes.

"For me, chainsaw carving is incredible fun—destruction, construction, and creativity all at work at once, and I love it. If I won the lottery tomorrow, I would still be doing what I'm doing today."

Part Three

Chainsaw Power Carving a Chair Step-by-Step

Now that you've read about the history of chainsaw carving and its most accomplished artists, perhaps you'd like to give the art form a try. A chair is a great beginning chainsaw carver's project; the basic form of a chair is easy to shape, and adding details only takes a bit of experience and creativity. Though a chair is functional, it can be a sculpture in and of itself. There are so many variations and nuances in design and style that it is easy to create your own. I have provided this totem-type chair to get you started.

The image of the bear is derived from the Pacific Northwest natives' art and woodcarvings. The people who lived in this soggy corner of North America long ago carved away at cedar logs and created divine renditions of the creatures in this area, real and mythical—bears, orcas, frogs, thunderbirds with their spread wings, and ravens. For the natives of the Northwest Coast, art was an intimate part of their culture, a part of everyday life as well as a part of ceremonial life.

The bear is the subject of many legends and superstitions and is often featured in artwork, particularly in totem poles, button blankets, spirit masks, and family crests. When it is represented in art, the bear has large, flaring nostrils, a wide mouth with teeth bared, and sometimes a protruding tongue. Sharp claws and feet are typical, and the tiny tail of the bear is generally ignored.

The Northwest Coast natives believe that the spirit of the bear is within all of us and that we must come to terms with it in our lives. For some, this myth extends to all of creation. Therefore, many of the Northwest Coast natives have a deep spiritual connection with bears.

So with this in mind, I would like to share with you, in western red cedar, the *Sun, Moon, Bear Chair*. The design is my own, based on inspirations of the art of the natives of the Pacific Northwest. The mask design on the chair back has a bear face in the center with the sun and the moon around its head. The red ring represents the sun; the blue represents the moon. The bear is one of the most powerful animals on earth in a natural, mythical, and spiritual sense. Enjoy yourself carving some aspect of the great grizzly bear's spirit. The bear may appear to be majestic, dangerous, or any other emotion that you wish to portray.

Tools and Materials

Saws
- Echo 346 with 8" dime-tip carving bar
- Husqvarna 346 XP with 18" stock bar

Other Tools and Supplies
- Orbital sander
- Angle grinder
- Diamond sander (optional)
- Die grinder with a round nose bit
- Die grinder with a dovetail router bit
- Hatchet, ax, pry bar, or slick
- Lumber crayon
- Safety chaps
- Ear and eye protection of choice
- Latex paints in red, blue, and white
- 1 qt. Danish oil
- 1 qt. marine spar varnish, satin finish, or satin wax

1

A 3' western red cedar log waiting to be turned into a chair. I chose a 20"-diameter log, but the wood can be bigger or smaller, depending on your personal preference.

2

Peel the bark off the log. Here I am using a hatchet and my hands, but you could use any blunt, edgy object, such as an axe, a pry bar, or a slick. Cedar is nice because its bark comes off in strands. By peeling the bark off, I find it saves me filing time on the chainsaw chain and helps to prevent the chain from wearing down so quickly.

3

The log is nice, clean, and ready to be carved.

4

I am measuring for the seat height of the chair; 18" is the standard chair height. Lumber crayons work well for marking logs.

5

Draw a vertical line and a horizontal line to define and guide the cuts that you will be making. I also drew a line on top of the log to help me visualize the cut.

6

Make the first cut by slicing down from the top of the log. I'm using a chainsaw with the 18" stock bar. I generally make this simple cut with the middle part of the saw, leveling it out as I continue cutting downward. Make sure you wear your safety chaps and ear and eye protection.

7

Side view of the chair. Notice the stance I'm using: my body is to the side of the saw.

8

The back side of the chair. I'm almost to the bottom of my mark.

9

Finish the first cut.

10 Start the perpendicular cut. Again, I start this cut by using the middle of the saw, leveling it as I continue on to my mark, or the first cut. This cut will free the block.

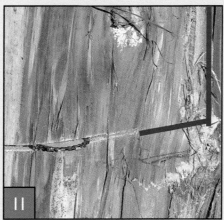

11 The red line shows the two cuts meeting. The piece is on its way to being free.

12 The block is free. The piece is already a chair in two simple cuts.

13 Level the high spots by cutting downward.

14 With gentle pressure, using the saw as a planer, skim it up and down the chair until the back is level.

15 Plane the seat as well, skimming it until it is level.

16 Using my off cut, I rest the chair against it to make the next cuts, the feet.

17 Mark the lines to show where the next cuts will go.

18 Start the first cut in the middle and continue downward until you reach the bottom. Be sure that you don't hit the ground because it will dull the saw immediately.

19 For the second cut, follow the angle that you drew. Using the tip of the bar with gentle pressure, safely submerge it into the wood until you meet the first cut. Then, continue on down. This will release a wedge shape. Do the same cut on the other line.

20 The result so far.

21 The back of the chair. I lean the front part of the chair on my off cut and do the same cuts on the back of the chair.

22 To create legs on the side, use the same method as you did on the front and the back. Do both sides. The inset shows the results so far.

23 The back view of the feet of the chair.

24 Round the corners of the back on one side . . .

25 . . . then round the corners on the other side.

26 A concave cut. First, cut down, and then round back.

27 Shown here is a different way to make the concave cut on the other side, using two cuts. Start at the top, about 4" from the seat, and cut down until you meet the seat. On the second cut, start about 3" to 4" away, and, using the upper part of the saw, continue forward until you meet the first cut. This will release a wedge-shaped piece of wood.

28

To make the feet prominent, start cutting downward in an arc, almost to the bottom, leaving enough wood for the bear's toes and claws—around 4".

29

Notice how the horizontal cut meets the first cut to release the wedge shape.

30

Remove the wedge shape. Then, level any high spots by gently skimming the surface.

31

Skim off about ¼" around the chair, taking off the surface wood. I use the edge of my saw, going downward.

32

Here is the progress to this point.

33

I drew the first rough sketch of where the mask will go on the chair back. Using the small saw with an 8" dime-tip carving bar, etch where you drew the lines.

34

Here I am etching the line on the other side, too. Go in about ¾".

35

After cutting the line, run the saw tip parallel to the chair back, meeting the cut you created to remove the wood.

36

The result so far.

37

Move down to the toes. Running the saw down, angled toward you, remove some wood to shape the toes.

38

Add toe/claw lines. Carve five toes for each foot. Do both sides.

39

Here, I've finished the first claw.

40

Make a horizontal cut to define the seat.

41

Continue the line until you reach the front part of the side of the chair.

42

Draw arms and clawed hands on both sides of the chair. Then, define the lines with the saw.

43

Cut in about ¾" deep.

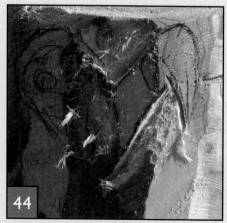

44

Scrape around the line with the saw, defining the arm further. Continue skimming and smoothing around the chair.

45

Trim the edges to give the seat back some shape.

46

Draw some decorative marks on the front of the legs and etch them out.

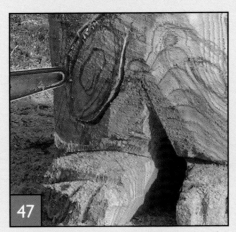

47

Cut a line on the outer circle as well as the inner circle of the decorative marks.

48

Use the skimming method to remove wood by running the saw and gently scraping back and forth.

49

Define the legs. Here, I am taking out wood with the tip of the saw. I remove wood until it looks pleasing to the eye. Keep in mind that this is a somewhat free-form chair, so there are no mistakes.

50

The chair so far.

51

Now we're ready to use the angle grinder. Using 36 grit, grind all of the high spots, smoothing and cleaning the surface of the chair. I spend about 10 minutes grinding with a light touch all over the chair. Redraw your design as necessary. I usually redraw my lines a few times throughout this sanding process.

52

Be very careful with the grinder, especially around edges like this; the grinder can catch and get away from you.

53

I continue lightly but firmly sanding the edge of the chair.

54

Notice the angle of the grinder to the wood. This is the angle I use to sand most of the chair because it is easier to control and it feels comfortable.

55 The chair after about 10 minutes of sanding with 36 grit.

56 Now, sand with 50 grit. Here, I'm touching up the toes.

57 Spend another 10 minutes with the 50 grit, sanding the whole chair.

58 After the chair is sanded, redraw the designs and lines where you're going to cut, such as the sides of the chair back.

59 Draw the sun/moon design, lightly defining the lines using a die grinder with a dovetail router bit. Carve in all of the lines that you drew with the dovetail router bit or with whatever works best for you.

60 Hold the die grinder so it allows the tip of the bit to carve into the line.

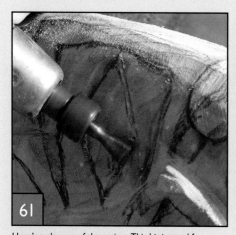

61 Here's a closeup of the action. This bit is good for carving thin lines.

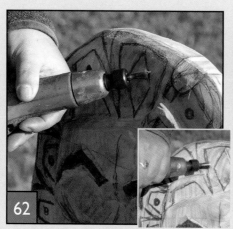

62 I often go back and forth among the chainsaw, the die grinder, and the angle grinder.

63 Here, I notice that it would be quicker to remove the wood inside the mouth of the grizzly and on the design elements with a chainsaw.

64

I use the round nose bit above the eye for gently removing and shaping wood at the same time.

65

Remove the wood in between the sunrays.

66

The results so far after using the round bit.

67

Using the angle grinder, sand the surface with 50 grit, cleaning up the high spots and leveling and smoothing the surface.

68

Touch up the lips, shaping and sanding.

69

The result after sanding with 50 grit.

70

Again, redraw the lines.

71

Work on the eyes with the dovetail router bit. I angle it in on the top part of the eyeball, undercutting into the eyelid.

72

Add lines in for teeth and on the nostrils and other places, as desired.

73 With the angle grinder, sand the chair with 80 grit.

74 Use the orbital sander with 120 grit, and sand the chair, reaching all the places that you can, even the top.

75 I use a sander with a diamond-shaped pad to reach the surfaces that were missed with the orbital sander.

76 Detail the eyeball with the dovetail router bit.

77 The chair is pretty much finished at this point. I usually go on to sand it either up to 180 grit or 240 grit depending on whether or not I plan to paint. (You need a smoother finish if you will not be painting your piece.) At this point, instead of finishing it off with the sanders, I decide to add another design element—a space, which opens up the chair back and gives it a different feel.

78 To create that space, first draw the design. The first cut is at an angle, starting at the base of the bear's chin, going down to the point, keeping the angle the whole way.

79 The second cut. The third cut will be at the chin, going from one side to the other, releasing the triangle shape.

80 The wood has been removed. Clean up the saw marks.

81 The final sanding. Now we're ready for paint and oil.

The chair after paint and oil. I used Danish oil and applied it three times, wet-dry sanding after each application with 320- then 400-grit sandpaper. If it's an indoor piece, top coat it with a satin wax. If it's an outdoor piece, use a satin marine spar varnish.

Gallery of Chainsaw Carved Chairs

I've included the following examples of my chairs to provide you with some ideas and inspiration for any future projects you might carve. Many are sculptural chairs that are about form, style, and showing off the color and grain of the wood. There are also several examples of sculptural animal chairs by Pat McVay.

Chair with Spine, western red cedar, 3' high by 2' wide.

Chair with Flair, western red cedar, 4½' high by 2½' wide.

Salmon Chair, redwood, 7' high by 4' wide.

Pat McVay made this set by cutting his log at a diagonal. Western red cedar with dark stain, 5' high by 3½' wide.

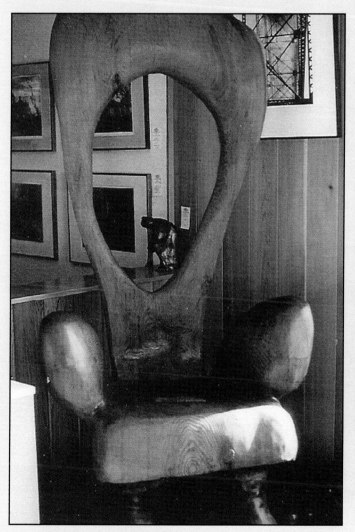

Portal Chair, redwood, 7' high by 3½' wide.

A chair with a television set for my entry at the Northern California Chainsaw Carving Contest in 1997. I did a similar set in the Shelton, Washington, contest in 1994.

Part Four

Chainsaw Carving Events, Yesterday and Today

Chainsaw carving shows and competitions have played an important role in the development of the art form. These events gathered artists together, exposing them to the different styles of the art. Shows and competitions also helped to create performance chainsaw art, which focuses on speed and on the interaction between the artist and his or her audience. The first shows emerged in the 1980s and became venues for artists to share ideas and push artistic limits.

Roadside attractions: paving the path for profits

Once carvers began using the chainsaw to create artwork, the question arose: "What do I do with all of these creations?" Rather than leave their newly formed sculptures to meld in their backyard, many decided to sell their wares. Shops sprung up along heavily traveled tourist roads and chainsaw carvers quickly learned that they could make a living selling their art.

One such roadside shop was Moore's Mountain Village, conveniently nestled near the entry to Mount Rainer, Washington's tallest mountain. Owner Duke Moore began carving humorous people and carousel animals in the 1950s. In an effort to promote his shop and gather carvers, Duke went on to organize one of the first chainsaw carving shows ever, which took place in 1980.

For other business-savvy chainsaw artists, such as Ray Kowalski, tourist attractions were the way to go. For a small fee, visitors could tour his small-scale theme park that featured humorous, chainsaw carved Western characters. These roadside attractions provided the groundwork for chainsaw carving events to come.

Fairs, logger shows, and grand openings: chainsaw carving becomes performance art

While many chainsaw carvers staked out permanent shops on the roadside, others took their art on the road. They found work with organizers at state fairs, logging shows, and shopping malls, who were eager to hire flamboyant chainsaw carvers to wow crowds. One of the first agencies to book chainsaw carvers was the Dean Short Talent Agency out of Iowa. They booked Jerry Ward in 1983 to perform at a state fair. The agency later hired A.J. Lutter who would perform three to four one-hour programs per day. Soon, groups of chainsaw carvers started carving together. This resulted in faster action, more drama, and amazed audiences. Today, marketers still look to chainsaw carvers for crowd-pleasing performances.

Vintage Chainsaw Contests

Carvers gather to exchange ideas and to compete

As chainsaw carving grew in popularity, carvers had a desire to get together to exchange ideas, to compete, and to view the work of other artists. In the 1980s, pioneering artists organized contests, symposiums, and shows to meet the growing demand. Although many of the early shows have died out, they paved the way for popular chainsaw shows today. Some shows, such as West Coast, The Big One! have sustained success over the years.

Moore's Mountain Village Chainsaw Carving Competition
1980–1992

Duke Moore, owner of Moore's Mountain Village in Ashford, Washington, organized one of the first chainsaw carving events ever to take place. He hosted the event at his roadside shop which featured his large collection of work ranging in size from six inches to six feet. Although there are not many photographs documenting the event, it was very a significant event for the growing number of chainsaw artists who attended. The show took place every summer for twelve years.

▲ A letter from Duke's Mountain Village inviting woodcarvers to come and carve. Photo courtesy Pat McVay

On The Road To Paradise • Mt Rainier

9th ANNUAL CHAIN SAW CARVING CHAMPIONSHIP

Dear Carvers,

Moores Mountain Village invites you to the 9th Annual Chain Saw Carving Championship at our village one mile east of Ashford on Highway 706. The dates are July 15th and 16th. We hope you can come and exchange ideas and just have some good old time fun.

The carving starts at 10:00 AM and runs until 6:00 PM both days. We will provide the logs so just bring your tools and saws. Prizes will be given to the top three contestants.

Please fill out the contestant form and send it to: **Moores Mountain Village, 31811 East SR 706, Box T, Ashford, WA 98304** no later than June 15, 1989. For more information please call 569-2251.

◀ Rob Chalk, the first Australian to compete in America, competed in Duke's competition. Photo by Pat McVay.

◀ Dave Sipe, the first Minnesotan to participate in a Washington event. Photo by Pat McVay.

▲ Susan Miller and Duke Moore with Duke's carvings. Photo by Pat McVay.

▲ Lynn Backus and her entry. She was one of the first ladies to compete in this event.

The First World Championships, Puyallup, WA
September 12, 1981

Legendary chainsaw carver, Mike McVay organized the first World Championships of Chainsaw Carving at the Western Washington State Fair. The event featured a totem pole contest in which carvers had six hours to carve a 12-inch-diameter, 20-foot-long totem pole. Carvers came from all over Washington and parts of Oregon to take part in the totem-themed event. Influential carvers in attendance included Steve Backus, Judy McVay, Pat McVay, Susan Miller, and John Steiner.

Bob Canterbury, winner of the first World Championships, definitely has something to smile about. Photo courtesy Pat McVay.

Finished 20' totems after a six hour chainsaw carving contest. What a feat! Photo by Pat McVay.

A group of totem poles from the contest in 1981. The second pole from the right was carved by Mike McVay; the middle pole was carved by Bob Canterbury; and the left pole was carved by Judy McVay. Photo courtesy Pat McVay.

Carving competitions reach the Midwest

U.S. Nationals, Grand Rapids, MN, 1983
The World Championships, Hill City, MN, 1986
North American Championships, Hinkley, MN, 1987

Until the early 1980s, the Pacific Northwest was considered to be the center of the chainsaw carving community. Soon, a new hub began to form. Three significant shows emerged from Minnesota in the 1980s: The U.S. Nationals, The North American Championships, and Minnesota's own version of the World Championships, the idea of Barre Pinskie. Carvers came from as far away as New Mexico, Michigan, South Dakota, and Indiana to compete.

A piece by Layton Kiblinger of Washington State for The World Championships in Hill City.

◀ A piece by Ray Murphy for The World Championships in Hill City.

◀ A piece by Dennis Roghair of Minnesota for The World Championships in Hill City.

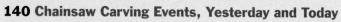

▲ Pat McVay's humor is evident with his entry for the North American Championships.

▲ A.J. Lutter and his carvings from the North American Championships held in Hinckley.

◀ A piece by Hal MacIntosh of New York for The North American Championships in Hinckley, Minnesota.

◀ Larry Jensen won the U.S. Nationals with this entry.

◀ A.J. Lutter with his first place carving, *Eagle Indian*, from the U.S. Nationals in 1988.

◀ A piece by Steve Backus of Washington for The North American Championships in Hinckley, Minnesota.

Today's major gatherings

Today, chainsaw carving shows and competitions continue to thrive. With expanding attendance figures and backing from national saw manufacturers these events are reaching new levels of success. Below is a look at two major events. The first event is West Coast, The Big One!, a world-class carving contest. The second, The Ridgway Rendezvous is the largest non-competitive chainsaw carving event in the country, with a deeper purpose.

Carvers, Wood and Money:
The Birth of The Big One!

Westport, Washington
Established in 1990

Before woodcarver Steve Backus dropped into the town of Westport, Washington, it was mainly known for fishing and surfing. Today, it is winning world-wide recognition for being home to the largest chainsaw competition.

The show was conceived in 1990 when the Backus family arrived in Westport for a vacation. Local motel owner, Jim McBroom spied Steve's truck full of carvings and offered him a room in exchange for a handsomely carved fish. Jim, who was intrigued by Steve's stories about the carving contest he had just attended asked, "What would it take to have a contest here?"

"Carvers, wood, and money," Steve replied. The two men came to a quick business agreement, and a new show was born. The show was aptly named, "The Big One!," and a date was set for August 1990. The first year, nine carvers converged on the small town and a $300 prize was awarded. The event grew, and the once not-so-big contest is now a world-class event, featuring up to 70 carvers from all over the world.

The contest is a physically grueling five-day event. At the end, five judges with backgrounds in woodcarving assess the work based on difficultly, craftsmanship, design, and state of completion. There is also a People's Choice Award which is decided by tallying up the individual ballots cast by spectators.

Although highly competitive, the show does have a softer side. It's an event where talented groups of artists are also friends. They share their equipment, loan saws, help each other move logs, and give each other pointers. "It's really a woodcarving seminar wrapped up in competition", says Backus.

▲ Conrad Sandoval works on his West Coast, The Big One! piece, *Jesus, from Darkness to Light*, 1998. Conrad has competed in many competitions on the West Coast and has won almost every one he has entered. Because Conrad is a minister, many of his pieces have religious themes.

▲ Jessie Groeschen in 2004. There are very few rules in West Coast, The Big One!—it's an open contest. The theme is nautical every year. All artists use a chainsaw for their roughing stages. Some carvers also use paint to brighten things up.

▲ Steve Backus, the founder of West Coast, The Big One!

▲ Boaz Backus, the brother of Steve, is another important part of this event. Multi-talented, Boaz not only carves, but also serves as the master of ceromines and auctioneer of this event. Since the event's inception, Boaz has been keeping the crowds informed. Photo by Ed Robinson.

▲ Pat McVay was Carvers' Choice Winner in 1990, when the carvers at The Big One! decided his was their favorite carving.

▲ Steve Backus, People's Choice Winner, 1990. In addition to organizing the event, Steve finds time to carve.

The Ridgway Chainsaw Carver's Rendezvous

Ridgway, Pennsylvania
Established in 1999

Now the largest non-competition-based chainsaw carving event, The Ridgway Chainsaw Carvers' Rendezvous was born in 1999 in the town of Ridgway, Pennsylvania. Rick and Randy Boni, the founders of the event, wanted a place where chainsaw carvers could carve, learn, interact with other carvers, and make a difference in the lives of others. Each year the sculptures are auctioned off, and some of the money is donated to both the Make-A-Wish-Foundation and the local YMCA.

The show started off with about 30 carvers in 1999. The next year, it doubled in size, and the community of Ridgway got more involved. In 2005, 215 carvers from nine countries around the world traveled to the town of Ridgway to share their passion for chainsaw carving, making this event the largest of its kind. The donations of carved pieces have raised $47,000 in 2004 and $42,000 in 2005 to benefit the charities.

▲ Rick Boni, who founded the Ridgway Rendezvous with his brother, Randy, is shown working in his Appalachian Art Studio in 2004.

▲ One of Rick's trademark pieces, *The Owl*, carved in 2004.

▲ Some of the carvers from Japan, enjoying a break from carving.

▲ Plaque by Judy McVay. Judy was honored that Rick and Liz Boni featured one of her murals for the 2005 T-shirt design. The participants, too, were honored to receive a shirt showing one of Judy's murals.

▲ *It's Never Too Cold to Wear a Bikini*, carved by Angela Polglaze, of Australia, in 2005. The piece measures 6' high and 2' wide.

▲ Eagle in cherry carved by Randy Boni for the first Rendezvous in 2000. Photo by Joe King.

▲ Zoë Boni, Rick's daughter, and her *Phoenix*.

◀ Joe King and *Arnold Palmer*, carved in pin oak in 2005, measuring 4' high and 2' wide. Joe spends much of his time during the Ridgway event picking up carvers and dropping them off at the airport. He is also a regular writer for *Chip Chats*. Although Joe did not create this piece at Ridgway, he himself is a regular and important fixture at the event.

International Events

Around the world: international chainsaw carving events

By the late 1980s, chainsaw carving events were springing up not just in the U.S. but also around the world—a clear sign that chainsaw carving was taking hold as an internationally recognized art form. Featured here are a few of the notable international contests, some of which are still taking place today.

Chainsaw Woodcarving Event, Iisalmi, Finland
Established 1987

Since 1987, a chainsaw carving event and contest near the center of Finland in the town of Iisalmi has been taking place. The carvers have twelve hours, spread over two days, to create their main, large piece. The event also features a quick carve.

Once the event is over, the carvers leave their pieces at Kolijonvirta Campground. Over the years, quite a collection of woodcarvings has accumulated for visitors to enjoy.

▲ A piece by Erkki Rytkonen that placed in the 1997 event.

▲ A piece by Timo Kareinen that placed in the 1997 event.

Japan Chainsaw Carving Championships, Toei, Japan
Established 2001

In 2001, Japan held its first chainsaw carving contest in Toei, Japan, organized by the Toei Chainsaw Carving Club. They developed the idea after hearing about the carving contests that were happening in the U.S. Intrigued by the events in the U.S., five Japanese carvers traveled to Westport, Washington, in 2001 to participate in West Coast, The Big One!, held during the month of August. Later that year in November, the Toei Chainsaw Carving Club held its own event, formatted after the West Coast event. Today, there are many chainsaw carving clubs in Japan taking the art form to new heights.

▲ Naito Wataru, the winner of the event, Pro Division, 2002.

▲ Mr. Tadashi Ito, 2002 president of the Toei Chainsaw Carving Club, presents the People's Choice Award. All of the trophies for the contest were designed and carved by Brian J. Ruth.

National Chainsaw Carving Competition, Seymour, Australia
Established 1994

Kevin Gilders started the National Chainsaw Carving Competition in Seymour, Australia, in 1994. The competition stemmed from Kevin's days as a demonstrator. His exciting work attracted a large crowd, including Stihl representative, Rick Bourke. Kevin convinced Rick that there were sufficient carvers around to warrant a chainsaw carving competition, and Rick agreed to sponsor it.

The contest was a two-day event where carvers would complete a masterpiece in nine hours using a 6' x 2' pine log. It also featured daily speed carving competitions. Australia native John Brady won the first four competitions, and his record still stands today.

John Brady and his version of Lionel Rose. Photo courtesy Kevin Gilders.

Kevin Gilders' interesting self portrait. Photo courtesy Kevin Gilders.

English Open Chainsaw Carving Competition, Norfolk, England
Established 2004

After carving at the Ridgway Rendezvous in 2000 and learning of other carvers' interest in carving in England, Dennis Heath organized the first English Open Chainsaw Carving Competition in 2004. Because he knew Mark Hulme, the organizer of Sandringham Craft Show, Dennis was able to incorporate the competition into the craft show. The Sandringham Craft Show is a yearly event held on the grounds of the Queen's estate, Sandringham. Ireland, the U.S., Australia, Japan, Germany, Sweden, and the U.K. were all represented at the first competition—making this a truly international event.

The carvers have two-and-a-half days to produce their main piece. Each day, they also perform a quick carve to entertain the spectators and to show off their skills in speed art. In 2004, Bob King won the judges' portion of the event, and Andrew Frost received the Highly Commended award.

England's Andrew Frost watches his wood spirit come to life. Photo by Uncle Ed Robinson.

Jayne Sparks applies the final touches to Puff, the Magic Dragon. Photo by Nayson Mali.

Shows and Contests

National Road Chainsaw Carving Festival,
Pittsburgh, PA
June
(814) 395-3569
www.confluencelionsw.org

Oregon Divisional Chainsaw Sculpting Championships,
Reedsport, OR
June, Father's Day Weekend
(800) 247-2155 or (541) 271-3495 (Reedsport/Winchester
Bay Chamber of Commerce)
cking464@comcast.net
www.odcsc.com

Ridgway Rendezvous, Ridgway, PA
February
info@chainsawrendezvous.org
www.chainsawrendezvous.org

Annual Chainsaw Carving on the Mighty Mississippi Event,
Clatt Adams Park, Quincy, IL
October
(217) 228-0574
loghog@adams.net

Annual Fall Carving Festival, Creston, OH
September/October
(330) 769-2610
fallcarvingfest@wmconnect.com
fallcarvingfestival.tripod.com

West Coast, The Big One!, Westport WA
(360) 579-3574
nono@whidbey.com

Annual Carrbridge Chainsaw Carving Event,
Carrbridge, Scotland
jonesbunk@aol.com
www.carvecarrbridge.com

English Open Chainsaw Competition, Sandringham, England
dennis.heath@bigfoot.com
www.englishopenchainsawcompetition.co.uk

Fall Festival Mid-Atlantic Chain Saw Carving Competition,
Forksville, PA
(570) 946-4160
sulchamc@expix.net
www.sullivanpachamber.com

Scandia Chainsaw Carve,
Scandia, PA
May
(814) 757-8491
evergreen@westpa.net (use "carver" in the title)

Masters of the Chainsaw Presents: Invitational Extreme Power
Carving Competition, Schnecksville, PA
June
1-888-CHAINSAW
www.mastersofthechainsaw.com

Sand and Sawdust Sculpting Contest,
Ocean Shores, WA
June
(360) 500-9358

Annual Logs to Frogs Chainsaw Carving Competition,
Milton-Freewater, OR
July
(541) 938-8236
mike.Watkins@milton-freewater-or.gov
www.muddyfrogwatercountry.com/events.php

Bibliography

Bellis, Mary. "Chainsaw, Chain Saws." About, Inc. http://
inventors.about.com/od/cstartinventions/a/Chainsaws.htm.

Oregon Cutting Systems Group, Blount, Inc. "Along the
Oregon Way." http://www.oregonchain.com/company/history.htm

Clubs and Guilds

Cascade Chainsaw Sculptors Guild,
Milton, WA
(360) 494-7700
deb@ccsg.info
www.ccsg.info

United Chainsaw Carvers Guild
www.uccg.org

Chainsaw Sculptors.com
(906) 265-9599
www.chainsawsculptors.com

Featured Artists

J. Chester Armstrong
Wildlife Artisans
PO Box 253
Sisters, OR 97759
(541) 549-9344
www.jchesterarmstrong.com

R. L. Blair
rlblairwoodcarving@sbcglobal.net
www.rlblair.com

Steve Blanchard
Blanchard Wood Sculpture
667 Hwy. 68
Salinas, CA 93908
(831) 484-0963
Fax (831) 484-0960
steve@blanchardwoodsculpture.com
www.blanchardwoodsculpture.com
www.itsyville.com

Don Colp
47409 Hwy. 58
Oakridge, OR 97492
(541) 782-3843

Edith Croft
c/o Fox Chapel Publishing
1970 Broad St.
East Petersburg, PA 17520
(717) 560-4703

Glenn Greensides
glenn@greensidesart.com
www.greensidesart.com

Jessie Groeschen
PO Box 577
Langley, WA 98260
jessie@groeschen.com
www.groeschen.com

Lois Hollingsworth
c/o Fox Chapel Publishing
1970 Broad St.
East Petersburg, PA 17520
(717) 560-4703

A. J. Lutter:
Come See What I Saw
A. J. Lutter's Chainsaw Gallery
16396 Hwy. 371
Brainerd, MN 56401
(218) 829-3844
shmoopie@brainerd.net

Judy McVay
PO Box 41
Deming, WA 98244
(360) 595-0518

Pat McVay
8000 Scatchet Head Rd.
Clinton, WA 98236
(360) 579-7811
pat@mcvaysculpture.com
www.mcvaysculpture.com

Mike McVay
PO Box 873460 (year-round)
Wasilla, AK 99687
(907) 376-2298 and (907) 232-6989
mikemcvay@whidbeystore.com
www.whidbeystore.com/mikemvay

Workshop/store location
(open year-round)
2202 McCallister Rd.
MP 45.1 Parks Hwy.
Wasilla, AK
malaska@mymailstation.com

PO Box 934 (winter)
Langley, WA 98260
mmcvay@mymailstation.com

Susan Miller
71233 Hwy. 47
Mist, OR 97016
(503) 755-2508
susanm@huppi.com

Ray Murphy
PO Box 5074
Ellsworth, ME 04605

Ben Risney
Ben Risney Woodcarving Studio
(610) 888-CARV (2278)

Dennis Roghair
Kettle River Carving Company
33496 Townline Rd.
Hinckley, MN 55037
(320) 384-6033
www.SculptureByRoghair.com

Brian Ruth
Brian J Ruth Sculptures
located in the Village of Jonas, PA
1-888-CHAINSAW
Fax (570) 722-4102
bruth@chainsaw.net
www.mastersofthechainsaw.com

More Great Project Books from Fox Chapel Publishing

Chainsaw Carving an Eagle
A Complete Step-by-step Guide
By Jamie Doeren and Dennis Roghair
$16.95
Soft Cover
1-56523-253-4
80 Pages
8.5" x 11"

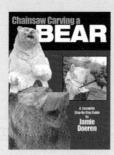

Chainsaw Carving a Bear
A Complete Step-by-step Guide
By Jamie Doeren
$16.95
Soft Cover
1-56523-183-X
72 Pages
8.5" x 11"

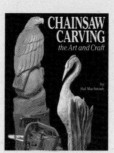

Chainsaw Carving The Art & Craft
By Hal Macintosh
$24.95
Soft Cover
1-56523-128-7
152 Pages
8.5" x 11"

Bear: The Ultimate Artist's Reference
By Doug Lindstrand
$19.95
Soft Cover
1-56523-214-3
120 Pages
8.5" x 11"

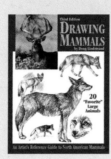

Drawing Mammals 3rd edition
An Artist's Reference Guide to North American Mammals
By Doug Lindstrand
$25
Soft Cover
1-56523-206-2
212 Pages
8.5" x 11"

Art of Stylized Wood Carving
By David Hamilton, Charles Solomon
$19.95
Soft Cover
1-56523-174-0
112 Pages
8.5" x 11"

LOOK FOR THESE BOOKS AT YOUR LOCAL BOOK STORE OR WOODWORKING RETAILER

Or call 800-457-9112 • Visit www.FoxChapelPublishing.com

Learn from the Experts

Fox Chapel Publishing is not only your leading resource for woodworking books, but also the publisher of the two leading how-to magazines for woodcarvers and woodcrafters!

WOOD CARVING ILLUSTRATED is the leading how-to magazine for woodcarvers of all skill levels and styles—providing inspiration and instruction from some of the world's leading carvers and teachers. A wide range of step-by-step projects are presented in an easy-to-follow format, with great photography and useful tips and techniques. *Wood Carving Illustrated* delivers quality editorial on the most popular carving styles, such as realistic and stylized wildlife carving, power carving, Santas, caricatures, chip carving and fine art carving. The magazine also includes tool reviews, painting and finishing features, profiles on carvers, photo galleries and more.

SCROLL SAW WORKSHOP is the leading how-to magazine for novice and professional woodcrafters. Shop-tested projects are complete with patterns and detailed instructions. The casual scroller appreciates the in-depth information that ensures success and yields results that are both useful and attractive; the pro will be creatively inspired with fresh and innovative design ideas. Each issue of *Scroll Saw Workshop* contains useful news, hints and tips, and includes lively features and departments that bring the world of scrolling to the reader.

Want to learn more about a subscription? Visit **www.FoxChapelPublishing.com** and click on either the *Wood Carving Illustrated* button or *Scroll Saw Workshop* button at the top of the page. Watch for our special **FREE ISSUE** offer! You can also write to us at 1970 Broad Street, East Petersburg, PA 17520 or call toll-free at 1-800-457-9112.